A Psalms Prayer Guide

Prayer is made easy when it is guided by

The Book of Psalms

By: David, Moses, Asaph, Heman, Jeduthun, Ethan, the Ezrahite, plus many unnamed authors.

Book I - Psalms 1 - 41   Book II - Psalms 42 - 72   Book III - Psalms 73 - 89
Book IV - Psalms 90 - 106   Book V-a - Psalms 107- 119
Book V-b - Psalms 120 - 134   Book V-c - Psalms 135 - 150

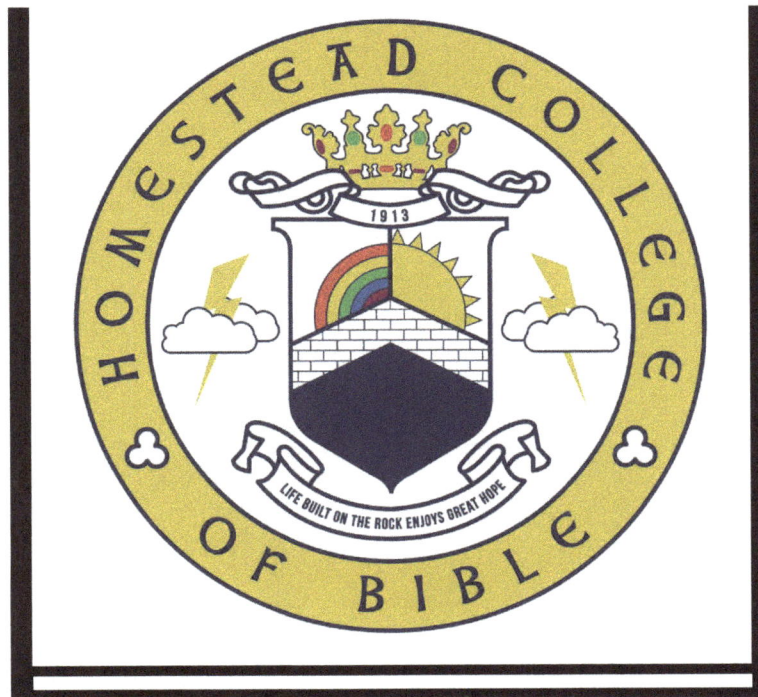

Paul Pent
Homestead College of Bible

This book belong to:

_____

Gabriel
by Michelle Robideaux-Pent

A Psalms Prayer Guide

Prayer is made easy when Prayer is guided by Psalms

Have you ever felt the need to spend a little time in prayer, so you got on your knees and started praying? Then, after 43 seconds, you could not find meaningful words with purpose.

Well, here is a helpful guide to allow you to be powerfully effective. But please do not look ahead and think "what a complicated code book." Just slowly nibble away at it and you will start to like it. It's like learning to pilot a plane. Take one little movement at a time and you will be amazed how it all comes together. Jesus said, "men aught always to pray and not to faint."

When you want to pray for ten solid minutes and not run out of things to say (or 30 minutes or an hour for that matter). Just go to whatever category of Psalms you desire.

This book has every Psalm identified with a category of prayer type. The Prayer types are:

1. **P** – Prayer - 7 Sub-types – **1.** Prayer of Prosperity and Stability, **2.** Peace and calm,

   3. Health / Cleansing, **4.** Spreading the Gospel, **5.** Fulfill promises for Kingdom's Glory, **6.** Save from enemies, **7.** Hear my Prayer and Teach

2. **B** – Blessing / Promise

3. **D** - Doctrine of God

4. **C** - Confession / Make Clear

5. **TSR** – Testimony of Salvation / Remembrance

6. **G** – Groaning

7. **W** – Worship / Praise

8. **M** – Messianic

9. **R** – Rebuke

10. **S** – Science / Supernatural

For example,
If you are asking for help, use one of the (P) Prayer designation. If you have a desire to know God better, use those identified as (D) Doctrine. When you need to repent for past sins, use (C) Confessions. If you wish to meditate on how God works for us, use the verse identified as (TSR) TSR – Testimony of God's Salvation / Remembrance.

The word <u>prayer</u> has two definitions in Scripture.

Definition of Prayer "A" is all communion with God including, request, worship, praise, confession, groaning, meditation in remembrance of His past works. An example is Psalms 90, Prayer of Moses, the Man of God.

Definition of Prayer "B" is simply a request.

There are some verses which have multiple types of prayer identification, but mostly only one identification is assigned to a verse. When you see a verse having more than one category, simply note to show the multiple categories. For example, when you are praising GOD, you will also see included within that a manifestation of Gods character (doctrine of God). **It is easy to pray.** Just pick the category that is fun for you! I am using the word "fun" lightly. Scripture does say "rejoice evermore." "In everything give thanks." When Job lost everything he said, "Should a living man complain?" Ultimately God gave him twice as much as he had before. Even groaning and confession of my sins will bring relief. Just try it.

Here are a few examples of categories you will find uplifting;

1. P.1   <u>Prosperity</u>: "save now I beseech thee O Lord, oh, Lord, I beseech thee send now prosperity" 118:25

     P.2 <u>Peace, and Calm</u>:" he maketh the storm, a calm, so that the waves thereof are still" 107:29

2. B   <u>Blessing and Promise</u>: "blessed is the man whom you choose, and causes to approach unto YOU" 65:4

3. D   <u>Doctrine</u>: "commit your way to the Lord, trust also in him, and he will bring it to pass" 37:5

4. C   <u>Confession</u>: "Have mercy on me, Oh God, for I am weak "6:2

5. TSR   TSR Testimony/<u>Remembrance</u>: "remember his marvelous works that he has done, his wonders, and the judgments of his mouth." 105:5

6. G   <u>Groaning</u>: "For my soul, is full of troubles, and my life draws near to the grave" 88:3

7. W   <u>Worship</u>:" From the rising of the sun to the going down of the same, The Lords name is to be praised. 113:3

8. M   <u>Messianic</u>: "My God, my God, why have you forsaken me" 22:1

9. R   <u>Rebuke</u>: "Why do the heathen rage, and the people imagine a vain thing…. against the Lord, and against his anointed."2:1&2

10. S   <u>Science</u> "He tells the number of the stars. He calls them all by their names." 147:4

Important Notes for Certain Categories:

1.P   Prayer

     " Fulfill promises for kingdoms glory" the Psalmist's request is for God to bring vengeance on the wicked. (these prayers are called imprecatory prayers) They are fulfilled through Christ, who said "vengeance is mine. I will repay says the Lord." So then our task is to "love our enemies,"and pray for God to destroy their wicked works Thus God destroys their wicked works(mostly through chastening) but brings our enemies into salvation.

2.B Blessing:

> #1. It is not a Prayer request, but a worship and confession of what is so when acted upon.
>
> (example: blessed is everyone that fears the lord; that walks in his ways 128:1)
>
> #2 When any faithful servant of the Lord projects, a biblical blessing on another, it is done "and
>
> they shall put my name on the children of Israel and I will bless them" Num.6:27

3. D Doctrine of God:
> As we look at the nature of God (who God is) we are changed into his image.
>
> 2 Cor 3:18

4. C Confession: There are about seven categories of confession. A few examples:
> #1 Naming a specific sin and asking mercy. 51:3
>
> #2 Not knowing a specific sin, but asking God to look deep and identify any wicked way, and
>
> then lead me 139:23&24
>
> #3 Acknowledging that we are a part of the sin of our nation 106:6 also Dan.9:4&5

5. TSR Remembering God's salvation: we are comforted, and our faith is increased seeing God's
> incredible variety of deliverance, even in the midst of our sin and rebellion. 78: Entire Chapter

6. G Groaning: Complaining is a sin, Num.11:1, but biblical groaning has a refreshment component.

7. W Worship: Jesus said "when you pray, say…"Our father, who art in heaven hallowed be your name
> "so then, the first thing after acknowledging him as your father is worship

Now read/meditate on all these worship verses, God is blessed, and he blesses you for blessing him.

8. M Messianic: These passages point to Christ and are fulfilled in Christ

9. R Rebuke: These are helpful passages that bring one to repentance or can be used to bring others to
> repentance. … Rebuke …with all long-suffering and doctrine l Tim.4:2

10. S Science: The Bible is not essentially a science book but when it touches on scientific fact, it's
> totally accurate.
>
> Example, 36:9. The human eye cannot see light until an external light sensitizes the retina.

This is an example using the Chart of *Psalms by Chapter and Verse*, which are listed on the following pages. The example is Psalm Chapter 80, verse 6. It is a Prayer 5 (P.5) verse. Meaning, the verse is a prayer of TSR, Testimony of Salvation and Remembrance, as listed above.

PSALM	80	6	P.5

Thou makest us a strife unto our neighbors: and our enemies laugh among themselves.

For each individual category all in one place, see the index on page 25

Oh, no it's the King James Version

So let's turn it into a modern translation
The "authorized version" is by far the most accurate translation. Let me help you do the unthinkable with just 10 word modification. You will sound 90% like you are reading an up to date translation.

This is the KJV word:
Knoweth, Heareth, /understandeth.
Ariseth, Bringeth, Speaketh, Seest

All the words ending in "St' or "eth", drop those letters
and replace with "s" (example: Knows, Hears, Speaks, etc.)

AS WRITTEN:	CHANGE TO:
Ye	You
Thou	You
Hast	Have
Whosoever	Whoever
Hath	Has
Shall	Will
Verily	Truly
Saith	Said
Unto	To

Three examples of a phrase:

1. Everyone who asketh receiveth.   Change to;   Everyone that asks receives. Matt. 7-8

2. For He knoweth vain men   For He knows vain men. Job 11:11

3. Whosoever will   Who ever will   Rev 22:176

When reading aloud you can make these changes as you go. When reading aloud it would help to mark ahead of time so it will flow with ease.

Now then, as you have grace, keep modifying these Old English words to simply be our simple English.

I pray this guide with provide you with the information to develop powerful prayer,
Paul Pent

For each individual category all in one place, see the index on page 25

Psalms Categories by Chapter and Verse

PSALM				PSALM				PSALM			
PSALM	1	1	B	PSALM	5	9	G	PSALM	8	7	D
PSALM	1	2	B	PSALM	5	9	W	PSALM	8	8	S
PSALM	1	3	B	PSALM	5	10	P.5	PSALM	8	9	W
PSALM	1	4	B	PSALM	5	11	P.5	PSALM	9	1	P.4
PSALM	1	5	B	PSALM	5	12	W	PSALM	9	1	W
PSALM	1	6	B	PSALM	6	1	P.2	PSALM	9	2	W
PSALM	2	1	R	PSALM	6	2	C	PSALM	9	3	W
PSALM	2	2	R	PSALM	6	3	G	PSALM	9	4	W
PSALM	2	3	R	PSALM	6	3	W	PSALM	9	5	W
PSALM	2	4	W	PSALM	6	4	G	PSALM	9	6	TSR
PSALM	2	5	W	PSALM	6	4	W	PSALM	9	7	D
PSALM	2	6	M	PSALM	6	5	G	PSALM	9	8	D
PSALM	2	7	M	PSALM	6	5	W	PSALM	9	9	D
PSALM	2	8	M	PSALM	6	6	G	PSALM	9	10	W
PSALM	2	8	P.4	PSALM	6	6	W	PSALM	9	11	D
PSALM	2	9	W	PSALM	6	7	G	PSALM	9	12	D
PSALM	2	10	R	PSALM	6	7	W	PSALM	9	13	P.6
PSALM	2	11	R	PSALM	6	8	G	PSALM	9	14	P.4
PSALM	2	12	B	PSALM	6	8	W	PSALM	9	14	W
PSALM	3	1	G	PSALM	6	9	G	PSALM	9	15	D
PSALM	3	2	W	PSALM	6	9	W	PSALM	9	16	D
PSALM	3	3	W	PSALM	6	10	G	PSALM	9	17	D
PSALM	3	4	TSR	PSALM	6	10	W	PSALM	9	18	D
PSALM	3	5	TSR	PSALM	7	1	G	PSALM	9	19	P.6
PSALM	3	6	TSR	PSALM	7	2	G	PSALM	9	20	P.5
PSALM	3	7	P.6	PSALM	7	3	G	PSALM	10	1	G
PSALM	3	7	TSR	PSALM	7	3	P.3	PSALM	10	2	D
PSALM	3	8	D	PSALM	7	4	P.3	PSALM	10	3	D
PSALM	4	1	P.7	PSALM	7	5	P.3	PSALM	10	4	D
PSALM	4	2	R	PSALM	7	6	P.6	PSALM	10	5	G
PSALM	4	3	D	PSALM	7	7	W	PSALM	10	5	W
PSALM	4	3	P.1	PSALM	7	8	W	PSALM	10	6	D
PSALM	4	3	R	PSALM	7	9	W	PSALM	10	7	D
PSALM	4	4	D	PSALM	7	10	D	PSALM	10	8	D
PSALM	4	4	P.1	PSALM	7	11	D	PSALM	10	9	D
PSALM	4	5	D	PSALM	7	12	D	PSALM	10	10	D
PSALM	4	5	P.1	PSALM	7	13	D	PSALM	10	11	D
PSALM	4	6	D	PSALM	7	14	D	PSALM	10	12	P.6
PSALM	4	6	R	PSALM	7	15	D	PSALM	10	13	D
PSALM	4	7	W	PSALM	7	16	D	PSALM	10	14	W
PSALM	4	8	W	PSALM	7	17	D	PSALM	10	15	P.5
PSALM	5	1	P.7	PSALM	8	1	D	PSALM	10	16	D
PSALM	5	2	P.7	PSALM	8	1	P.4	PSALM	10	17	W
PSALM	5	3	W	PSALM	8	1	W	PSALM	10	18	W
PSALM	5	4	W	PSALM	8	2	W	PSALM	11	1	TSR
PSALM	5	5	W	PSALM	8	3	W	PSALM	11	2	D
PSALM	5	6	W	PSALM	8	4	D	PSALM	11	3	G
PSALM	5	7	W	PSALM	8	5	D	PSALM	11	4	D
PSALM	5	8	P.7	PSALM	8	6	D	PSALM	11	5	D

P.1 Prosperity P.2 Peace P.3 Health P.4 Spread Gospel P.5 Fill Promises P.6 Save from Enemies P.7 Hear my Prayer B – Blessing D - Doctrine C - Confession TSR – Salvation G – Groaning W – Worship M – Messianic R – Rebuke S – Science

Psalms Categories by Chapter and Verse

PSALM	11	6	D	PSALM	17	5	P.1	PSALM	18	38	TSR
PSALM	11	7	D	PSALM	17	6	P.7	PSALM	18	39	TSR
PSALM	12	1	P.2	PSALM	17	7	P.1	PSALM	18	40	W
PSALM	12	2	P.2	PSALM	17	8	P.2	PSALM	18	41	D
PSALM	12	3	D	PSALM	17	9	P.2	PSALM	18	42	TSR
PSALM	12	4	D	PSALM	17	10	TSR	PSALM	18	43	W
PSALM	12	5	D	PSALM	17	11	TSR	PSALM	18	44	TSR
PSALM	12	6	D	PSALM	17	12	TSR	PSALM	18	45	TSR
PSALM	12	7	P.2	PSALM	17	13	P.6	PSALM	18	46	TSR
PSALM	12	7	W	PSALM	17	14	P.6	PSALM	18	47	TSR
PSALM	12	8	D	PSALM	17	15	W	PSALM	18	48	TSR
PSALM	13	1	G	PSALM	18	1	TSR	PSALM	18	49	W
PSALM	13	2	G	PSALM	18	2	TSR	PSALM	18	50	TSR
PSALM	13	3	P.7	PSALM	18	3	TSR	PSALM	19	1	S
PSALM	13	4	P.6	PSALM	18	4	TSR	PSALM	19	2	S
PSALM	13	5	W	PSALM	18	5	TSR	PSALM	19	3	S
PSALM	13	6	D	PSALM	18	6	TSR	PSALM	19	4	TSR
PSALM	13	6	W	PSALM	18	7	D	PSALM	19	5	TSR
PSALM	14	1	D	PSALM	18	8	D	PSALM	19	6	TSR
PSALM	14	2	D	PSALM	18	9	D	PSALM	19	7	D
PSALM	14	3	D	PSALM	18	10	D	PSALM	19	8	D
PSALM	14	4	D	PSALM	18	11	D	PSALM	19	9	D
PSALM	14	4	D	PSALM	18	12	D	PSALM	19	10	D
PSALM	14	5	TSR	PSALM	18	13	D	PSALM	19	11	D
PSALM	14	6	TSR	PSALM	18	14	D	PSALM	19	12	C
PSALM	14	7	TSR	PSALM	18	15	D	PSALM	19	12	P.3
PSALM	15	1	W	PSALM	18	15	W	PSALM	19	13	P.3
PSALM	15	2	D	PSALM	18	16	TSR	PSALM	19	14	P.7
PSALM	15	3	D	PSALM	18	17	TSR	PSALM	20	1	B
PSALM	15	4	D	PSALM	18	18	TSR	PSALM	20	1	P.7
PSALM	15	5	D	PSALM	18	19	TSR	PSALM	20	2	B
PSALM	16	1	P.3	PSALM	18	20	TSR	PSALM	20	3	B
PSALM	16	2	W	PSALM	18	21	TSR	PSALM	20	4	B
PSALM	16	3	P.1	PSALM	18	22	TSR	PSALM	20	5	P.7
PSALM	16	3	W	PSALM	18	23	TSR	PSALM	20	5	W
PSALM	16	4	TSR	PSALM	18	24	TSR	PSALM	20	6	D
PSALM	16	5	W	PSALM	18	25	W	PSALM	20	6	P.7
PSALM	16	6	TSR	PSALM	18	26	W	PSALM	20	7	TSR
PSALM	16	7	TSR	PSALM	18	27	W	PSALM	20	8	TSR
PSALM	16	8	TSR	PSALM	18	28	W	PSALM	20	9	P.2
PSALM	16	9	TSR	PSALM	18	29	W	PSALM	21	1	W
PSALM	16	10	M	PSALM	18	30	D	PSALM	21	2	M
PSALM	16	10	W	PSALM	18	31	D	PSALM	21	3	M
PSALM	16	11	M	PSALM	18	32	D	PSALM	21	4	M
PSALM	16	11	W	PSALM	18	33	D	PSALM	21	5	M
PSALM	17	1	P.7	PSALM	18	34	D	PSALM	21	6	M
PSALM	17	2	P.7	PSALM	18	35	W	PSALM	21	7	TSR
PSALM	17	3	W	PSALM	18	36	W	PSALM	21	8	W
PSALM	17	4	W	PSALM	18	37	TSR	PSALM	21	9	W

P.1 Prosperity P.2 Peace P.3 Health P.4 Spread Gospel P.5 Fill Promises P.6 Save from Enemies
P.7 Hear my Prayer B – Blessing D - Doctrine C - Confession TSR – Salvation G – Groaning W –
Worship M – Messianic R – Rebuke S – Science

PSALM	21	10	W	PSALM	24	2	S	PSALM	27	1	TSR
PSALM	21	11	M	PSALM	24	3	D	PSALM	27	2	TSR
PSALM	21	12	M	PSALM	24	4	D	PSALM	27	3	TSR
PSALM	21	13	M	PSALM	24	5	D	PSALM	27	4	TSR
PSALM	21	13	P.5	PSALM	24	6	D	PSALM	27	5	TSR
PSALM	22	1	M	PSALM	24	7	W	PSALM	27	6	TSR
PSALM	22	2	M	PSALM	24	8	W	PSALM	27	7	P.7
PSALM	22	3	M	PSALM	24	9	W	PSALM	27	8	TSR
PSALM	22	3	W	PSALM	24	10	D	PSALM	27	9	P.7
PSALM	22	4	TSR	PSALM	25	1	P.6	PSALM	27	10	TSR
PSALM	22	5	TSR	PSALM	25	1	W	PSALM	27	11	P.7
PSALM	22	6	G	PSALM	25	2	P.6	PSALM	27	12	P.6
PSALM	22	6	M	PSALM	25	3	P.6	PSALM	27	13	TSR
PSALM	22	7	G	PSALM	25	4	P.7	PSALM	27	14	D
PSALM	22	7	M	PSALM	25	5	P.7	PSALM	28	1	P.7
PSALM	22	8	M	PSALM	25	6	P.1	PSALM	28	2	P.7
PSALM	22	8	W	PSALM	25	7	C	PSALM	28	3	P.6
PSALM	22	9	M	PSALM	25	7	P.3	PSALM	28	4	P.6
PSALM	22	9	W	PSALM	25	8	D	PSALM	28	5	D
PSALM	22	10	W	PSALM	25	9	D	PSALM	28	6	W
PSALM	22	11	P.2	PSALM	25	10	D	PSALM	28	7	W
PSALM	22	12	G	PSALM	25	11	C	PSALM	28	8	W
PSALM	22	12	M	PSALM	25	11	P.3	PSALM	28	9	P.1
PSALM	22	13	M	PSALM	25	12	D	PSALM	29	1	D
PSALM	22	14	M	PSALM	25	13	D	PSALM	29	2	D
PSALM	22	15	M	PSALM	25	14	D	PSALM	29	3	D
PSALM	22	16	M	PSALM	25	15	W	PSALM	29	4	D
PSALM	22	17	M	PSALM	25	16	P.3	PSALM	29	5	D
PSALM	22	18	M	PSALM	25	17	P.4	PSALM	29	6	D
PSALM	22	19	P.2	PSALM	25	18	C	PSALM	29	7	D
PSALM	22	20	P.6	PSALM	25	18	P.3	PSALM	29	8	D
PSALM	22	21	P.6	PSALM	25	19	P.6	PSALM	29	9	D
PSALM	22	22	M	PSALM	25	20	P.3	PSALM	29	10	D
PSALM	22	23	D	PSALM	25	21	P.1	PSALM	29	11	D
PSALM	22	24	TSR	PSALM	25	22	P.2	PSALM	30	1	W
PSALM	22	25	TSR	PSALM	26	1	P.1	PSALM	30	2	TSR
PSALM	22	26	D	PSALM	26	1	W	PSALM	30	3	TSR
PSALM	22	27	D	PSALM	26	2	C	PSALM	30	4	TSR
PSALM	22	28	D	PSALM	26	2	P.2	PSALM	30	5	D
PSALM	22	29	D	PSALM	26	3	TSR	PSALM	30	6	TSR
PSALM	22	30	D	PSALM	26	4	TSR	PSALM	30	7	TSR
PSALM	22	31	D	PSALM	26	5	TSR	PSALM	30	8	TSR
PSALM	23	1	TSR	PSALM	26	6	TSR	PSALM	30	9	TSR
PSALM	23	2	TSR	PSALM	26	7	TSR	PSALM	30	10	P.7
PSALM	23	3	TSR	PSALM	26	8	TSR	PSALM	30	10	TSR
PSALM	23	4	W	PSALM	26	9	P.6	PSALM	30	11	TSR
PSALM	23	5	W	PSALM	26	10	P.6	PSALM	30	12	TSR
PSALM	23	6	W	PSALM	26	11	P.2	PSALM	31	1	P.7
PSALM	24	1	W	PSALM	26	12	TSR	PSALM	31	2	P.7

P.1 Prosperity P.2 Peace P.3 Health P.4 Spread Gospel P.5 Fill Promises P.6 Save from Enemies P.7 Hear my Prayer B – Blessing D - Doctrine C - Confession TSR – Salvation G – Groaning W – Worship M – Messianic R – Rebuke S – Science

PSALM	31	3	P.2	PSALM	33	17	D	PSALM	35	21	G
PSALM	31	4	P.1	PSALM	33	18	D	PSALM	35	22	P.6
PSALM	31	5	M	PSALM	33	19	D	PSALM	35	23	P.6
PSALM	31	6	TSR	PSALM	33	20	TSR	PSALM	35	24	P.6
PSALM	31	7	TSR	PSALM	33	21	TSR	PSALM	35	25	P.6
PSALM	31	8	TSR	PSALM	33	22	P.2	PSALM	35	26	P.6
PSALM	31	9	P.3	PSALM	34	1	W	PSALM	35	27	W
PSALM	31	10	W	PSALM	34	2	W	PSALM	35	28	W
PSALM	31	11	G	PSALM	34	3	D	PSALM	36	1	D
PSALM	31	12	G	PSALM	34	4	TSR	PSALM	36	2	D
PSALM	31	13	G	PSALM	34	5	TSR	PSALM	36	3	D
PSALM	31	14	TSR	PSALM	34	6	TSR	PSALM	36	4	D
PSALM	31	15	P.6	PSALM	34	7	D	PSALM	36	5	D
PSALM	31	16	P.2	PSALM	34	8	D	PSALM	36	5	W
PSALM	31	17	P.6	PSALM	34	9	D	PSALM	36	6	D
PSALM	31	18	P.6	PSALM	34	10	D	PSALM	36	6	W
PSALM	31	19	P.6	PSALM	34	11	D	PSALM	36	7	D
PSALM	31	20	TSR	PSALM	34	12	D	PSALM	36	7	W
PSALM	31	21	TSR	PSALM	34	13	D	PSALM	36	8	D
PSALM	31	22	TSR	PSALM	34	14	D	PSALM	36	8	W
PSALM	31	23	D	PSALM	34	15	D	PSALM	36	9	D
PSALM	31	24	D	PSALM	34	16	D	PSALM	36	9	S
PSALM	32	1	W	PSALM	34	17	D	PSALM	36	9	W
PSALM	32	2	W	PSALM	34	18	D	PSALM	36	10	P.1
PSALM	32	3	G	PSALM	34	19	D	PSALM	36	11	P.1
PSALM	32	4	G	PSALM	34	20	D	PSALM	36	12	D
PSALM	32	5	C	PSALM	34	20	M	PSALM	37	1	D
PSALM	32	6	W	PSALM	34	21	D	PSALM	37	2	D
PSALM	32	7	TSR	PSALM	34	22	D	PSALM	37	3	D
PSALM	32	8	D	PSALM	35	1	P.6	PSALM	37	4	D
PSALM	32	9	D	PSALM	35	2	P.6	PSALM	37	5	D
PSALM	32	10	D	PSALM	35	3	P.6	PSALM	37	6	D
PSALM	32	11	D	PSALM	35	4	P.6	PSALM	37	7	D
PSALM	33	1	D	PSALM	35	5	P.6	PSALM	37	8	D
PSALM	33	2	D	PSALM	35	6	P.6	PSALM	37	9	D
PSALM	33	3	D	PSALM	35	7	P.6	PSALM	37	10	D
PSALM	33	4	D	PSALM	35	8	P.6	PSALM	37	11	D
PSALM	33	5	D	PSALM	35	9	W	PSALM	37	12	D
PSALM	33	6	D	PSALM	35	10	W	PSALM	37	13	D
PSALM	33	7	D	PSALM	35	11	M	PSALM	37	14	D
PSALM	33	8	D	PSALM	35	12	G	PSALM	37	15	D
PSALM	33	9	D	PSALM	35	13	G	PSALM	37	16	D
PSALM	33	10	D	PSALM	35	14	G	PSALM	37	17	D
PSALM	33	11	D	PSALM	35	15	G	PSALM	37	18	D
PSALM	33	12	D	PSALM	35	16	G	PSALM	37	19	D
PSALM	33	13	D	PSALM	35	17	P.6	PSALM	37	20	D
PSALM	33	14	D	PSALM	35	18	W	PSALM	37	21	D
PSALM	33	15	D	PSALM	35	19	P.6	PSALM	37	22	D
PSALM	33	16	D	PSALM	35	20	G	PSALM	37	23	D

P.1 Prosperity P.2 Peace P.3 Health P.4 Spread Gospel P.5 Fill Promises P.6 Save from Enemies
P.7 Hear my Prayer B – Blessing D - Doctrine C - Confession TSR – Salvation G – Groaning W –
Worship M – Messianic R – Rebuke S – Science

Psalms Categories by Chapter and Verse

PSALM	37	24	D	PSALM	39	1	TSR	PSALM	41	11	M
PSALM	37	25	D	PSALM	39	2	M	PSALM	41	12	G
PSALM	37	26	D	PSALM	39	3	TSR	PSALM	41	12	M
PSALM	37	27	D	PSALM	39	4	P.3	PSALM	41	13	W
PSALM	37	28	D	PSALM	39	5	P.3	PSALM	42	1	W
PSALM	37	29	D	PSALM	39	6	D	PSALM	42	2	W
PSALM	37	30	D	PSALM	39	7	P.3	PSALM	42	3	G
PSALM	37	31	D	PSALM	39	8	C	PSALM	42	4	TSR
PSALM	37	32	D	PSALM	39	8	P.3	PSALM	42	5	G
PSALM	37	33	D	PSALM	39	9	M	PSALM	42	5	W
PSALM	37	34	D	PSALM	39	10	P.3	PSALM	42	6	G
PSALM	37	35	D	PSALM	40	1	TSR	PSALM	42	6	W
PSALM	37	36	D	PSALM	40	2	TSR	PSALM	42	7	G
PSALM	37	37	D	PSALM	40	3	TSR	PSALM	42	7	W
PSALM	37	38	D	PSALM	40	4	TSR	PSALM	42	8	W
PSALM	37	39	D	PSALM	40	5	M	PSALM	42	9	G
PSALM	37	40	D	PSALM	40	5	W	PSALM	42	9	W
PSALM	38	1	C	PSALM	40	6	M	PSALM	42	10	G
PSALM	38	1	G	PSALM	40	7	M	PSALM	42	10	W
PSALM	38	2	C	PSALM	40	8	TSR	PSALM	42	11	G
PSALM	38	2	G	PSALM	40	9	TSR	PSALM	42	11	W
PSALM	38	3	C	PSALM	40	10	TSR	PSALM	43	1	P.6
PSALM	38	3	G	PSALM	40	11	P.3	PSALM	43	2	G
PSALM	38	4	C	PSALM	40	12	G	PSALM	43	3	P.7
PSALM	38	4	G	PSALM	40	13	P.3	PSALM	43	4	TSR
PSALM	38	5	C	PSALM	40	14	P.6	PSALM	43	5	G
PSALM	38	5	G	PSALM	40	15	P.6	PSALM	44	1	TSR
PSALM	38	6	C	PSALM	40	16	P.4	PSALM	44	2	TSR
PSALM	38	6	G	PSALM	40	17	G	PSALM	44	3	TSR
PSALM	38	7	C	PSALM	40	17	P.2	PSALM	44	4	P.6
PSALM	38	7	G	PSALM	40	17	TSR	PSALM	44	5	TSR
PSALM	38	8	C	PSALM	40	17	W	PSALM	44	6	TSR
PSALM	38	8	G	PSALM	41	1	B	PSALM	44	7	TSR
PSALM	38	8	M	PSALM	41	2	B	PSALM	44	8	TSR
PSALM	38	9	M	PSALM	41	3	B	PSALM	44	9	G
PSALM	38	10	M	PSALM	41	4	C	PSALM	44	10	G
PSALM	38	11	M	PSALM	41	5	G	PSALM	44	11	G
PSALM	38	12	M	PSALM	41	5	M	PSALM	44	12	G
PSALM	38	13	M	PSALM	41	6	G	PSALM	44	13	G
PSALM	38	14	M	PSALM	41	6	M	PSALM	44	14	G
PSALM	38	15	M	PSALM	41	7	G	PSALM	44	15	G
PSALM	38	16	M	PSALM	41	7	M	PSALM	44	16	G
PSALM	38	17	M	PSALM	41	8	G	PSALM	44	17	TSR
PSALM	38	18	C	PSALM	41	8	M	PSALM	44	18	TSR
PSALM	38	18	M	PSALM	41	9	G	PSALM	44	19	TSR
PSALM	38	19	M	PSALM	41	9	M	PSALM	44	20	TSR
PSALM	38	20	M	PSALM	41	10	G	PSALM	44	21	D
PSALM	38	21	M	PSALM	41	10	M	PSALM	44	22	D
PSALM	38	22	M	PSALM	41	11	G	PSALM	44	23	P.6

P.1 Prosperity P.2 Peace P.3 Health P.4 Spread Gospel P.5 Fill Promises P.6 Save from Enemies P.7 Hear my Prayer B – Blessing D - Doctrine C - Confession TSR – Salvation G – Groaning W – Worship M – Messianic R – Rebuke S – Science

Psalms Categories by Chapter and Verse

PSALM	44	24	G	PSALM	46	9	W	PSALM	49	3	TSR
PSALM	44	25	G	PSALM	46	10	D	PSALM	49	4	D
PSALM	44	26	P.6	PSALM	46	10	W	PSALM	49	5	D
PSALM	45	1	TSR	PSALM	46	11	D	PSALM	49	6	D
PSALM	45	2	W	PSALM	46	11	W	PSALM	49	7	D
PSALM	45	3	W	PSALM	47	1	D	PSALM	49	8	D
PSALM	45	4	W	PSALM	47	1	W	PSALM	49	9	D
PSALM	45	5	W	PSALM	47	2	D	PSALM	49	10	D
PSALM	45	6	D	PSALM	47	2	W	PSALM	49	11	D
PSALM	45	6	M	PSALM	47	3	D	PSALM	49	12	D
PSALM	45	6	W	PSALM	47	3	W	PSALM	49	13	D
PSALM	45	7	M	PSALM	47	4	D	PSALM	49	14	D
PSALM	45	7	W	PSALM	47	4	W	PSALM	49	15	D
PSALM	45	8	W	PSALM	47	5	D	PSALM	49	15	W
PSALM	45	9	D	PSALM	47	5	W	PSALM	49	16	D
PSALM	45	9	W	PSALM	47	6	D	PSALM	49	17	D
PSALM	45	10	D	PSALM	47	6	W	PSALM	49	18	D
PSALM	45	10	W	PSALM	47	7	D	PSALM	49	19	D
PSALM	45	11	D	PSALM	47	7	W	PSALM	49	20	D
PSALM	45	11	W	PSALM	47	8	D	PSALM	50	1	D
PSALM	45	12	D	PSALM	47	8	W	PSALM	50	1	W
PSALM	45	12	W	PSALM	47	9	D	PSALM	50	2	D
PSALM	45	13	D	PSALM	47	9	W	PSALM	50	2	W
PSALM	45	13	W	PSALM	48	1	D	PSALM	50	3	D
PSALM	45	14	D	PSALM	48	1	W	PSALM	50	3	W
PSALM	45	14	W	PSALM	48	2	D	PSALM	50	4	D
PSALM	45	15	D	PSALM	48	2	W	PSALM	50	4	W
PSALM	45	15	W	PSALM	48	3	D	PSALM	50	5	D
PSALM	45	16	D	PSALM	48	3	W	PSALM	50	5	W
PSALM	45	16	W	PSALM	48	4	D	PSALM	50	6	D
PSALM	45	17	D	PSALM	48	4	W	PSALM	50	6	W
PSALM	45	17	W	PSALM	48	5	D	PSALM	50	7	D
PSALM	46	1	D	PSALM	48	5	W	PSALM	50	8	D
PSALM	46	1	W	PSALM	48	6	D	PSALM	50	9	D
PSALM	46	2	D	PSALM	48	6	W	PSALM	50	10	D
PSALM	46	2	W	PSALM	48	7	D	PSALM	50	11	D
PSALM	46	3	D	PSALM	48	7	W	PSALM	50	12	D
PSALM	46	3	W	PSALM	48	8	D	PSALM	50	13	D
PSALM	46	4	D	PSALM	48	8	W	PSALM	50	14	D
PSALM	46	4	W	PSALM	48	9	TSR	PSALM	50	14	G
PSALM	46	5	D	PSALM	48	10	TSR	PSALM	50	15	D
PSALM	46	5	W	PSALM	48	11	P.7	PSALM	50	16	D
PSALM	46	6	D	PSALM	48	12	D	PSALM	50	17	D
PSALM	46	6	W	PSALM	48	13	D	PSALM	50	18	D
PSALM	46	7	D	PSALM	48	14	D	PSALM	50	19	D
PSALM	46	7	W	PSALM	49	1	D	PSALM	50	20	D
PSALM	46	8	D	PSALM	49	2	D	PSALM	50	21	D
PSALM	46	8	W	PSALM	49	3	D	PSALM	50	22	D
PSALM	46	9	D	PSALM	49	3	M	PSALM	50	23	D

P.1 Prosperity P.2 Peace P.3 Health P.4 Spread Gospel P.5 Fill Promises P.6 Save from Enemies
P.7 Hear my Prayer B – Blessing D - Doctrine C - Confession TSR – Salvation G – Groaning W –
Worship M – Messianic R – Rebuke S – Science

PSALM	50	23	G	PSALM	55	3	G	PSALM	57	10	TSR
PSALM	51	1	P.3	PSALM	55	4	G	PSALM	57	11	P.4
PSALM	51	2	P.3	PSALM	55	5	G	PSALM	58	1	R
PSALM	51	3	C	PSALM	55	6	G	PSALM	58	2	R
PSALM	51	4	D	PSALM	55	7	G	PSALM	58	3	D
PSALM	51	5	D	PSALM	55	8	G	PSALM	58	4	D
PSALM	51	6	D	PSALM	55	9	P.6	PSALM	58	5	D
PSALM	51	7	P.3	PSALM	55	10	G	PSALM	58	6	P.5
PSALM	51	8	P.2	PSALM	55	11	G	PSALM	58	7	P.5
PSALM	51	9	C	PSALM	55	12	G	PSALM	58	8	P.5
PSALM	51	9	P.3	PSALM	55	12	M	PSALM	58	9	D
PSALM	51	10	C	PSALM	55	13	G	PSALM	58	10	D
PSALM	51	10	P.3	PSALM	55	13	M	PSALM	58	12	D
PSALM	51	11	C	PSALM	55	14	G	PSALM	59	1	P.6
PSALM	51	11	P.2	PSALM	55	14	M	PSALM	59	2	P.6
PSALM	51	12	C	PSALM	55	15	P.5	PSALM	59	3	P.6
PSALM	51	12	P.2	PSALM	55	16	TSR	PSALM	59	4	P.6
PSALM	51	13	P.4	PSALM	55	17	TSR	PSALM	59	5	P.6
PSALM	51	14	C	PSALM	55	18	TSR	PSALM	59	6	P.6
PSALM	51	14	P.4	PSALM	55	19	D	PSALM	59	7	P.6
PSALM	51	15	P.4	PSALM	55	20	D	PSALM	59	8	W
PSALM	51	16	P.2	PSALM	55	21	D	PSALM	59	9	W
PSALM	51	17	P.2	PSALM	55	21	D	PSALM	59	10	W
PSALM	51	18	P.2	PSALM	55	21	D	PSALM	59	11	P.6
PSALM	51	19	D	PSALM	55	22	D	PSALM	59	12	P.6
PSALM	52	1	R	PSALM	55	23	D	PSALM	59	13	P.6
PSALM	52	2	R	PSALM	55	23	D	PSALM	59	14	P.6
PSALM	52	3	R	PSALM	56	1	P.6	PSALM	59	15	P.6
PSALM	52	4	R	PSALM	56	2	P.6	PSALM	59	16	TSR
PSALM	52	5	R	PSALM	56	3	P.2	PSALM	59	17	TSR
PSALM	52	6	D	PSALM	56	4	W	PSALM	60	1	G
PSALM	52	7	D	PSALM	56	5	G	PSALM	60	2	G
PSALM	52	8	D	PSALM	56	6	G	PSALM	60	3	G
PSALM	52	9	W	PSALM	56	7	P.5	PSALM	60	4	W
PSALM	53	1	D	PSALM	56	8	G	PSALM	60	5	P.6
PSALM	53	2	D	PSALM	56	9	W	PSALM	60	6	W
PSALM	53	3	D	PSALM	56	10	TSR	PSALM	60	7	W
PSALM	53	4	D	PSALM	56	11	TSR	PSALM	60	8	W
PSALM	53	5	TSR	PSALM	56	12	TSR	PSALM	60	9	W
PSALM	53	6	TSR	PSALM	56	13	TSR	PSALM	60	10	W
PSALM	54	1	P.7	PSALM	57	1	P.2	PSALM	60	11	P.1
PSALM	54	2	G	PSALM	57	2	TSR	PSALM	60	12	W
PSALM	54	3	P.6	PSALM	57	3	D	PSALM	61	1	P.7
PSALM	54	4	P.6	PSALM	57	4	G	PSALM	61	2	P.7
PSALM	54	5	P.6	PSALM	57	5	P.5	PSALM	61	3	P.7
PSALM	54	6	TSR	PSALM	57	6	G	PSALM	61	4	P.7
PSALM	54	7	TSR	PSALM	57	7	TSR	PSALM	61	5	P.7
PSALM	55	1	G	PSALM	57	8	TSR	PSALM	61	5	W
PSALM	55	2	G	PSALM	57	9	TSR	PSALM	61	6	W

P.1 Prosperity P.2 Peace P.3 Health P.4 Spread Gospel P.5 Fill Promises P.6 Save from Enemies P.7 Hear my Prayer B – Blessing D - Doctrine C - Confession TSR – Salvation G – Groaning W – Worship M – Messianic R – Rebuke S – Science

PSALM				PSALM				PSALM			
PSALM	61	7	W	PSALM	65	10	W	PSALM	68	11	TSR
PSALM	61	8	W	PSALM	65	11	W	PSALM	68	12	TSR
PSALM	62	1	W	PSALM	65	12	W	PSALM	68	13	D
PSALM	62	2	W	PSALM	65	13	W	PSALM	68	14	TSR
PSALM	62	3	R	PSALM	66	1	D	PSALM	68	15	D
PSALM	62	4	R	PSALM	66	1	W	PSALM	68	16	D
PSALM	62	5	C	PSALM	66	2	D	PSALM	68	17	D
PSALM	62	5	W	PSALM	66	2	W	PSALM	68	18	TSR
PSALM	62	6	D	PSALM	66	3	D	PSALM	68	19	W
PSALM	62	7	D	PSALM	66	3	W	PSALM	68	20	D
PSALM	62	8	D	PSALM	66	4	D	PSALM	68	21	D
PSALM	62	9	D	PSALM	66	4	W	PSALM	68	22	D
PSALM	62	10	D	PSALM	66	5	D	PSALM	68	23	D
PSALM	62	11	D	PSALM	66	5	W	PSALM	68	24	TSR
PSALM	62	12	W	PSALM	66	6	D	PSALM	68	25	TSR
PSALM	63	1	W	PSALM	66	6	W	PSALM	68	26	W
PSALM	63	2	W	PSALM	66	7	D	PSALM	68	27	W
PSALM	63	3	W	PSALM	66	7	W	PSALM	68	28	P.1
PSALM	63	4	W	PSALM	66	8	W	PSALM	68	29	W
PSALM	63	5	W	PSALM	66	9	W	PSALM	68	30	P.5
PSALM	63	6	W	PSALM	66	10	W	PSALM	68	31	D
PSALM	63	7	W	PSALM	66	11	W	PSALM	68	32	D
PSALM	63	8	W	PSALM	66	12	W	PSALM	68	33	D
PSALM	63	9	W	PSALM	66	13	W	PSALM	68	34	D
PSALM	63	10	W	PSALM	66	14	W	PSALM	68	35	W
PSALM	63	11	W	PSALM	66	15	W	PSALM	69	1	P.2
PSALM	64	1	P.7	PSALM	66	16	W	PSALM	69	2	G
PSALM	64	2	G	PSALM	66	17	TSR	PSALM	69	3	G
PSALM	64	3	G	PSALM	66	18	D	PSALM	69	4	G
PSALM	64	4	G	PSALM	66	19	TSR	PSALM	69	5	C
PSALM	64	5	G	PSALM	66	20	W	PSALM	69	5	W
PSALM	64	6	G	PSALM	67	1	P.4	PSALM	69	6	P.7
PSALM	64	7	D	PSALM	67	2	P.4	PSALM	69	7	G
PSALM	64	8	D	PSALM	67	3	P.4	PSALM	69	8	G
PSALM	64	9	D	PSALM	67	4	P.4	PSALM	69	9	M
PSALM	64	10	D	PSALM	67	5	P.4	PSALM	69	10	G
PSALM	65	1	W	PSALM	67	6	P.4	PSALM	69	11	G
PSALM	65	2	W	PSALM	67	7	P.4	PSALM	69	12	G
PSALM	65	3	C	PSALM	68	1	P.5	PSALM	69	13	W
PSALM	65	3	G	PSALM	68	2	P.5	PSALM	69	14	P.6
PSALM	65	3	W	PSALM	68	3	D	PSALM	69	15	P.6
PSALM	65	4	B	PSALM	68	3	P.2	PSALM	69	16	P.6
PSALM	65	4	W	PSALM	68	4	D	PSALM	69	17	P.6
PSALM	65	5	W	PSALM	68	5	D	PSALM	69	18	P.6
PSALM	65	6	D	PSALM	68	6	D	PSALM	69	19	G
PSALM	65	6	W	PSALM	68	7	W	PSALM	69	20	G
PSALM	65	7	W	PSALM	68	8	TSR	PSALM	69	21	M
PSALM	65	8	W	PSALM	68	9	TSR	PSALM	69	22	P.6
PSALM	65	9	W	PSALM	68	10	TSR	PSALM	69	23	P.6

P.1 Prosperity P.2 Peace P.3 Health P.4 Spread Gospel P.5 Fill Promises P.6 Save from Enemies
P.7 Hear my Prayer B – Blessing D - Doctrine C - Confession TSR – Salvation G – Groaning W –
Worship M – Messianic R – Rebuke S – Science

PSALM	69	24	P.6	PSALM	72	8	D	PSALM	73	20	W
PSALM	69	25	P.6	PSALM	72	9	D	PSALM	73	21	G
PSALM	69	26	G	PSALM	72	10	D	PSALM	73	22	G
PSALM	69	27	P.6	PSALM	72	11	D	PSALM	73	23	G
PSALM	69	28	P.6	PSALM	72	12	D	PSALM	73	24	G
PSALM	69	29	P.1	PSALM	72	13	D	PSALM	73	25	G
PSALM	69	30	TSR	PSALM	72	14	D	PSALM	73	26	G
PSALM	69	31	TSR	PSALM	72	15	D	PSALM	73	27	G
PSALM	69	32	D	PSALM	72	16	D	PSALM	73	28	D
PSALM	69	33	D	PSALM	72	17	M	PSALM	74	1	G
PSALM	69	34	W	PSALM	72	18	W	PSALM	74	2	P.7
PSALM	69	35	D	PSALM	72	19	W	PSALM	74	3	P.7
PSALM	69	36	D	PSALM	72	20	D	PSALM	74	4	G
PSALM	70	1	P.6	PSALM	73	1	D	PSALM	74	5	G
PSALM	70	2	P.6	PSALM	73	1	G	PSALM	74	6	G
PSALM	70	3	P.6	PSALM	73	2	D	PSALM	74	7	G
PSALM	70	4	P.6	PSALM	73	2	G	PSALM	74	8	G
PSALM	70	5	P.6	PSALM	73	3	D	PSALM	74	9	G
PSALM	71	1	P.7	PSALM	73	3	G	PSALM	74	10	G
PSALM	71	2	P.6	PSALM	73	4	D	PSALM	74	11	G
PSALM	71	3	P.6	PSALM	73	4	G	PSALM	74	12	TSR
PSALM	71	4	P.6	PSALM	73	5	D	PSALM	74	13	TSR
PSALM	71	5	W	PSALM	73	5	G	PSALM	74	14	TSR
PSALM	71	6	W	PSALM	73	6	D	PSALM	74	15	TSR
PSALM	71	7	W	PSALM	73	6	G	PSALM	74	16	TSR
PSALM	71	8	P.4	PSALM	73	7	D	PSALM	74	17	TSR
PSALM	71	9	P.3	PSALM	73	7	G	PSALM	74	18	P.6
PSALM	71	10	P.6	PSALM	73	8	D	PSALM	74	19	P.6
PSALM	71	11	P.6	PSALM	73	8	G	PSALM	74	20	P.7
PSALM	71	12	P.6	PSALM	73	9	D	PSALM	74	21	P.6
PSALM	71	13	P.6	PSALM	73	9	G	PSALM	74	22	P.6
PSALM	71	14	TSR	PSALM	73	10	D	PSALM	74	23	P.6
PSALM	71	15	TSR	PSALM	73	10	G	PSALM	75	1	W
PSALM	71	16	TSR	PSALM	73	11	D	PSALM	75	2	TSR
PSALM	71	17	W	PSALM	73	11	G	PSALM	75	3	D
PSALM	71	18	P.4	PSALM	73	12	D	PSALM	75	4	TSR
PSALM	71	19	W	PSALM	73	12	G	PSALM	75	5	D
PSALM	71	20	W	PSALM	73	13	D	PSALM	75	6	D
PSALM	71	21	W	PSALM	73	13	G	PSALM	75	7	D
PSALM	71	22	W	PSALM	73	14	D	PSALM	75	8	TSR
PSALM	71	23	TSR	PSALM	73	14	G	PSALM	75	9	TSR
PSALM	71	24	TSR	PSALM	73	15	D	PSALM	75	10	TSR
PSALM	72	1	P.1	PSALM	73	15	G	PSALM	76	1	D
PSALM	72	2	D	PSALM	73	16	D	PSALM	76	2	D
PSALM	72	3	D	PSALM	73	16	G	PSALM	76	3	D
PSALM	72	4	D	PSALM	73	17	D	PSALM	76	4	W
PSALM	72	5	D	PSALM	73	17	W	PSALM	76	5	D
PSALM	72	6	D	PSALM	73	18	W	PSALM	76	6	W
PSALM	72	7	D	PSALM	73	19	W	PSALM	76	7	W

P.1 Prosperity P.2 Peace P.3 Health P.4 Spread Gospel P.5 Fill Promises P.6 Save from Enemies P.7 Hear my Prayer B – Blessing D - Doctrine C - Confession TSR – Salvation G – Groaning W – Worship M – Messianic R – Rebuke S – Science

PSALM	76	8	TSR	PSALM	78	15	D	PSALM	78	39	D
PSALM	76	9	TSR	PSALM	78	15	TSR	PSALM	78	39	TSR
PSALM	76	10	D	PSALM	78	16	D	PSALM	78	40	D
PSALM	76	11	D	PSALM	78	16	TSR	PSALM	78	40	TSR
PSALM	76	12	D	PSALM	78	17	D	PSALM	78	41	D
PSALM	77	1	TSR	PSALM	78	17	TSR	PSALM	78	41	TSR
PSALM	77	2	TSR	PSALM	78	18	D	PSALM	78	42	D
PSALM	77	3	TSR	PSALM	78	18	TSR	PSALM	78	42	TSR
PSALM	77	4	G	PSALM	78	19	D	PSALM	78	43	D
PSALM	77	5	TSR	PSALM	78	19	TSR	PSALM	78	43	TSR
PSALM	77	6	TSR	PSALM	78	20	D	PSALM	78	44	D
PSALM	77	7	G	PSALM	78	20	TSR	PSALM	78	44	TSR
PSALM	77	8	G	PSALM	78	21	D	PSALM	78	45	D
PSALM	77	9	G	PSALM	78	21	TSR	PSALM	78	45	TSR
PSALM	77	10	TSR	PSALM	78	22	D	PSALM	78	46	D
PSALM	77	11	TSR	PSALM	78	22	TSR	PSALM	78	46	TSR
PSALM	77	12	TSR	PSALM	78	23	D	PSALM	78	47	D
PSALM	77	13	W	PSALM	78	23	TSR	PSALM	78	47	TSR
PSALM	77	14	W	PSALM	78	24	D	PSALM	78	48	D
PSALM	77	15	TSR	PSALM	78	24	TSR	PSALM	78	48	TSR
PSALM	77	16	TSR	PSALM	78	25	D	PSALM	78	49	D
PSALM	77	17	TSR	PSALM	78	25	S	PSALM	78	49	TSR
PSALM	77	18	TSR	PSALM	78	25	TSR	PSALM	78	50	D
PSALM	77	19	W	PSALM	78	26	D	PSALM	78	50	TSR
PSALM	77	20	TSR	PSALM	78	26	TSR	PSALM	78	51	D
PSALM	78	1	D	PSALM	78	27	D	PSALM	78	51	TSR
PSALM	78	2	TSR	PSALM	78	27	TSR	PSALM	78	52	D
PSALM	78	3	TSR	PSALM	78	28	D	PSALM	78	52	TSR
PSALM	78	4	TSR	PSALM	78	28	TSR	PSALM	78	53	D
PSALM	78	5	D	PSALM	78	29	D	PSALM	78	53	TSR
PSALM	78	5	TSR	PSALM	78	29	TSR	PSALM	78	54	D
PSALM	78	6	D	PSALM	78	30	D	PSALM	78	54	TSR
PSALM	78	6	TSR	PSALM	78	30	TSR	PSALM	78	55	D
PSALM	78	7	D	PSALM	78	31	D	PSALM	78	55	TSR
PSALM	78	7	TSR	PSALM	78	31	TSR	PSALM	78	56	D
PSALM	78	8	D	PSALM	78	32	D	PSALM	78	56	TSR
PSALM	78	8	TSR	PSALM	78	32	TSR	PSALM	78	57	D
PSALM	78	9	D	PSALM	78	33	D	PSALM	78	57	TSR
PSALM	78	9	TSR	PSALM	78	33	TSR	PSALM	78	58	D
PSALM	78	10	D	PSALM	78	34	D	PSALM	78	58	TSR
PSALM	78	10	TSR	PSALM	78	34	TSR	PSALM	78	59	D
PSALM	78	11	D	PSALM	78	35	D	PSALM	78	59	TSR
PSALM	78	11	TSR	PSALM	78	35	TSR	PSALM	78	60	D
PSALM	78	12	D	PSALM	78	36	D	PSALM	78	60	TSR
PSALM	78	12	TSR	PSALM	78	36	TSR	PSALM	78	61	D
PSALM	78	13	D	PSALM	78	37	D	PSALM	78	61	TSR
PSALM	78	13	TSR	PSALM	78	37	TSR	PSALM	78	62	D
PSALM	78	14	D	PSALM	78	38	D	PSALM	78	62	TSR
PSALM	78	14	TSR	PSALM	78	38	TSR	PSALM	78	63	D

P.1 Prosperity P.2 Peace P.3 Health P.4 Spread Gospel P.5 Fill Promises P.6 Save from Enemies
P.7 Hear my Prayer B – Blessing D - Doctrine C - Confession TSR – Salvation G – Groaning W –
Worship M – Messianic R – Rebuke S – Science

Psalms Categories by Chapter and Verse

PSALM	78	63	TSR	PSALM	80	11	TSR	PSALM	83	16	P.5
PSALM	78	64	D	PSALM	80	12	G	PSALM	83	17	P.5
PSALM	78	64	TSR	PSALM	80	13	G	PSALM	83	18	P.5
PSALM	78	65	D	PSALM	80	14	P.5	PSALM	84	2	W
PSALM	78	65	TSR	PSALM	80	15	P.5	PSALM	84	3	W
PSALM	78	66	D	PSALM	80	16	G	PSALM	84	4	W
PSALM	78	66	TSR	PSALM	80	17	P.5	PSALM	84	5	W
PSALM	78	67	D	PSALM	80	18	TSR	PSALM	84	6	W
PSALM	78	67	TSR	PSALM	80	19	P.5	PSALM	84	7	D
PSALM	78	68	D	PSALM	81	1	W	PSALM	84	7	W
PSALM	78	68	TSR	PSALM	81	2	W	PSALM	84	8	P.7
PSALM	78	69	D	PSALM	81	3	W	PSALM	84	8	W
PSALM	78	69	TSR	PSALM	81	4	TSR	PSALM	84	9	W
PSALM	78	70	D	PSALM	81	5	TSR	PSALM	84	10	W
PSALM	78	70	TSR	PSALM	81	6	TSR	PSALM	84	11	W
PSALM	78	71	D	PSALM	81	7	TSR	PSALM	84	12	W
PSALM	78	71	TSR	PSALM	81	8	TSR	PSALM	85	1	TSR
PSALM	78	72	D	PSALM	81	9	TSR	PSALM	85	2	TSR
PSALM	78	72	TSR	PSALM	81	10	TSR	PSALM	85	3	TSR
PSALM	79	1	G	PSALM	81	11	TSR	PSALM	85	4	G
PSALM	79	2	G	PSALM	81	12	TSR	PSALM	85	5	G
PSALM	79	3	G	PSALM	81	13	TSR	PSALM	85	6	P.1
PSALM	79	4	G	PSALM	81	14	TSR	PSALM	85	7	D
PSALM	79	5	G	PSALM	81	15	D	PSALM	85	7	P.1
PSALM	79	6	G	PSALM	81	16	D	PSALM	85	8	D
PSALM	79	7	G	PSALM	82	1	D	PSALM	85	9	D
PSALM	79	8	C	PSALM	82	2	R	PSALM	85	10	D
PSALM	79	8	G	PSALM	82	3	D	PSALM	85	11	D
PSALM	79	8	P.3	PSALM	82	4	D	PSALM	85	12	D
PSALM	79	9	C	PSALM	82	5	S	PSALM	85	13	D
PSALM	79	9	G	PSALM	82	6	TSR	PSALM	86	1	P.7
PSALM	79	9	P.3	PSALM	82	7	TSR	PSALM	86	2	P.7
PSALM	79	10	G	PSALM	82	8	P.5	PSALM	86	3	P.7
PSALM	79	10	P.4	PSALM	83	1	P.5	PSALM	86	4	P.2
PSALM	79	11	G	PSALM	83	1	W	PSALM	86	5	W
PSALM	79	11	P.2	PSALM	83	2	P.5	PSALM	86	6	P.7
PSALM	79	12	G	PSALM	83	3	P.5	PSALM	86	7	TSR
PSALM	79	12	P.5	PSALM	83	4	P.5	PSALM	86	8	W
PSALM	79	13	TSR	PSALM	83	5	P.5	PSALM	86	9	W
PSALM	80	1	P.5	PSALM	83	6	P.5	PSALM	86	10	W
PSALM	80	2	P.5	PSALM	83	7	P.5	PSALM	86	11	P.7
PSALM	80	3	P.5	PSALM	83	8	P.5	PSALM	86	12	W
PSALM	80	4	G	PSALM	83	9	P.5	PSALM	86	13	W
PSALM	80	5	G	PSALM	83	10	P.5	PSALM	86	14	G
PSALM	80	6	P.5	PSALM	83	11	P.5	PSALM	86	15	W
PSALM	80	7	P.5	PSALM	83	12	P.5	PSALM	86	16	P.1
PSALM	80	8	TSR	PSALM	83	13	P.5	PSALM	86	17	P.2
PSALM	80	9	TSR	PSALM	83	14	P.5	PSALM	87	1	D
PSALM	80	10	TSR	PSALM	83	15	P.5	PSALM	87	2	D

P.1 Prosperity P.2 Peace P.3 Health P.4 Spread Gospel P.5 Fill Promises P.6 Save from Enemies P.7 Hear my Prayer B – Blessing D - Doctrine C - Confession TSR – Salvation G – Groaning W – Worship M – Messianic R – Rebuke S – Science

Psalms Categories by Chapter and Verse

PSALM	87	3	W	PSALM	89	27	TSR	PSALM	91	1	D
PSALM	87	4	TSR	PSALM	89	28	TSR	PSALM	91	2	TSR
PSALM	87	5	D	PSALM	89	29	TSR	PSALM	91	3	D
PSALM	87	6	D	PSALM	89	30	TSR	PSALM	91	4	D
PSALM	87	7	D	PSALM	89	31	TSR	PSALM	91	5	D
PSALM	88	1	G	PSALM	89	32	TSR	PSALM	91	6	D
PSALM	88	2	P.7	PSALM	89	33	TSR	PSALM	91	7	D
PSALM	88	3	G	PSALM	89	34	TSR	PSALM	91	8	D
PSALM	88	4	G	PSALM	89	35	TSR	PSALM	91	9	D
PSALM	88	5	G	PSALM	89	36	TSR	PSALM	91	10	D
PSALM	88	6	G	PSALM	89	37	G	PSALM	91	11	D
PSALM	88	7	G	PSALM	89	38	G	PSALM	91	12	D
PSALM	88	8	G	PSALM	89	39	G	PSALM	91	13	D
PSALM	88	9	G	PSALM	89	40	G	PSALM	91	14	TSR
PSALM	88	10	P.4	PSALM	89	41	G	PSALM	91	15	TSR
PSALM	88	11	P.4	PSALM	89	42	G	PSALM	91	16	TSR
PSALM	88	12	TSR	PSALM	89	43	G	PSALM	92	1	D
PSALM	88	13	G	PSALM	89	44	G	PSALM	92	2	W
PSALM	88	14	G	PSALM	89	45	G	PSALM	92	3	W
PSALM	88	15	G	PSALM	89	46	P.4	PSALM	92	4	W
PSALM	88	16	G	PSALM	89	47	P.2	PSALM	92	5	W
PSALM	88	17	G	PSALM	89	48	P.2	PSALM	92	6	W
PSALM	88	18	G	PSALM	89	49	P.2	PSALM	92	7	W
PSALM	89	1	W	PSALM	89	50	P.2	PSALM	92	8	W
PSALM	89	2	W	PSALM	89	51	P.2	PSALM	92	9	W
PSALM	89	3	M	PSALM	89	52	W	PSALM	92	10	W
PSALM	89	4	M	PSALM	90	1	W	PSALM	92	11	W
PSALM	89	5	W	PSALM	90	2	W	PSALM	92	12	D
PSALM	89	6	W	PSALM	90	3	D	PSALM	92	13	D
PSALM	89	7	W	PSALM	90	3	W	PSALM	92	14	D
PSALM	89	8	W	PSALM	90	4	D	PSALM	92	15	D
PSALM	89	9	W	PSALM	90	4	W	PSALM	92	15	TSR
PSALM	89	10	W	PSALM	90	5	W	PSALM	93	1	D
PSALM	89	11	W	PSALM	90	6	W	PSALM	93	2	W
PSALM	89	12	W	PSALM	90	7	G	PSALM	93	3	W
PSALM	89	13	TSR	PSALM	90	7	W	PSALM	93	4	W
PSALM	89	14	W	PSALM	90	8	G	PSALM	93	5	W
PSALM	89	15	B	PSALM	90	8	W	PSALM	94	1	P.5
PSALM	89	16	W	PSALM	90	9	G	PSALM	94	2	P.5
PSALM	89	17	W	PSALM	90	9	W	PSALM	94	3	P.5
PSALM	89	18	W	PSALM	90	10	D	PSALM	94	4	P.5
PSALM	89	19	W	PSALM	90	10	W	PSALM	94	5	G
PSALM	89	20	W	PSALM	90	11	W	PSALM	94	6	G
PSALM	89	21	W	PSALM	90	12	P.3	PSALM	94	7	G
PSALM	89	22	W	PSALM	90	13	P.3	PSALM	94	8	R
PSALM	89	23	W	PSALM	90	14	P.3	PSALM	94	9	R
PSALM	89	24	M	PSALM	90	15	P.1	PSALM	94	10	R
PSALM	89	25	TSR	PSALM	90	16	P.1	PSALM	94	11	D
PSALM	89	26	TSR	PSALM	90	17	P.1	PSALM	94	12	W

P.1 Prosperity P.2 Peace P.3 Health P.4 Spread Gospel P.5 Fill Promises P.6 Save from Enemies
P.7 Hear my Prayer B – Blessing D - Doctrine C - Confession TSR – Salvation G – Groaning W – Worship M – Messianic R – Rebuke S – Science

PSALM	94	13	W	PSALM	97	2	D	PSALM	99	8	D
PSALM	94	14	D	PSALM	97	2	W	PSALM	99	8	W
PSALM	94	15	D	PSALM	97	3	D	PSALM	99	9	D
PSALM	94	16	G	PSALM	97	3	W	PSALM	99	9	W
PSALM	94	17	D	PSALM	97	4	D	PSALM	100	1	D
PSALM	94	18	W	PSALM	97	4	W	PSALM	100	1	W
PSALM	94	19	W	PSALM	97	5	D	PSALM	100	2	D
PSALM	94	20	W	PSALM	97	5	W	PSALM	100	2	W
PSALM	94	21	W	PSALM	97	6	D	PSALM	100	3	D
PSALM	94	22	W	PSALM	97	6	W	PSALM	100	3	W
PSALM	94	23	W	PSALM	97	7	D	PSALM	100	4	D
PSALM	95	1	W	PSALM	97	7	W	PSALM	100	4	W
PSALM	95	2	W	PSALM	97	8	D	PSALM	100	5	D
PSALM	95	3	D	PSALM	97	9	D	PSALM	100	5	W
PSALM	95	3	W	PSALM	97	10	D	PSALM	101	1	W
PSALM	95	4	D	PSALM	97	11	D	PSALM	101	2	G
PSALM	95	4	W	PSALM	97	12	D	PSALM	101	3	C
PSALM	95	5	D	PSALM	98	1	D	PSALM	101	4	C
PSALM	95	5	W	PSALM	98	1	W	PSALM	101	5	C
PSALM	95	6	D	PSALM	98	2	D	PSALM	101	6	TSR
PSALM	95	6	W	PSALM	98	2	W	PSALM	101	7	TSR
PSALM	95	7	D	PSALM	98	3	D	PSALM	101	8	TSR
PSALM	95	7	W	PSALM	98	3	W	PSALM	102	1	P.7
PSALM	95	8	D	PSALM	98	4	D	PSALM	102	2	P.7
PSALM	95	9	D	PSALM	98	4	W	PSALM	102	3	G
PSALM	95	10	D	PSALM	98	5	D	PSALM	102	4	G
PSALM	95	11	D	PSALM	98	5	W	PSALM	102	5	G
PSALM	96	1	D	PSALM	98	6	D	PSALM	102	6	G
PSALM	96	1	W	PSALM	98	6	W	PSALM	102	7	G
PSALM	96	2	D	PSALM	98	7	D	PSALM	102	8	G
PSALM	96	2	W	PSALM	98	7	W	PSALM	102	9	G
PSALM	96	3	D	PSALM	98	8	D	PSALM	102	10	G
PSALM	96	3	W	PSALM	98	8	W	PSALM	102	11	G
PSALM	96	4	D	PSALM	98	9	D	PSALM	102	12	W
PSALM	96	4	W	PSALM	98	9	W	PSALM	102	13	TSR
PSALM	96	5	D	PSALM	99	1	D	PSALM	102	14	TSR
PSALM	96	5	W	PSALM	99	1	W	PSALM	102	15	TSR
PSALM	96	6	D	PSALM	99	2	D	PSALM	102	16	TSR
PSALM	96	6	W	PSALM	99	2	W	PSALM	102	17	TSR
PSALM	96	7	D	PSALM	99	3	D	PSALM	102	18	TSR
PSALM	96	7	W	PSALM	99	3	W	PSALM	102	19	TSR
PSALM	96	8	D	PSALM	99	4	D	PSALM	102	20	TSR
PSALM	96	9	D	PSALM	99	4	W	PSALM	102	21	TSR
PSALM	96	10	D	PSALM	99	5	D	PSALM	102	22	TSR
PSALM	96	11	D	PSALM	99	5	W	PSALM	102	23	G
PSALM	96	12	D	PSALM	99	6	D	PSALM	102	24	G
PSALM	96	13	D	PSALM	99	6	W	PSALM	102	25	D
PSALM	97	1	D	PSALM	99	7	D	PSALM	102	25	M
PSALM	97	1	W	PSALM	99	7	W	PSALM	102	26	M

P.1 Prosperity P.2 Peace P.3 Health P.4 Spread Gospel P.5 Fill Promises P.6 Save from Enemies P.7 Hear my Prayer B – Blessing D - Doctrine C - Confession TSR – Salvation G – Groaning W – Worship M – Messianic R – Rebuke S – Science

Psalms Categories by Chapter and Verse

PSALM				PSALM				PSALM			
PSALM	102	27	M	PSALM	103	18	D	PSALM	104	20	D
PSALM	102	28	W	PSALM	103	18	W	PSALM	104	20	W
PSALM	103	1	B	PSALM	103	19	B	PSALM	104	21	D
PSALM	103	1	W	PSALM	103	19	D	PSALM	104	21	W
PSALM	103	2	B	PSALM	103	19	W	PSALM	104	22	D
PSALM	103	2	W	PSALM	103	20	B	PSALM	104	22	W
PSALM	103	3	B	PSALM	103	20	W	PSALM	104	23	D
PSALM	103	3	W	PSALM	103	21	B	PSALM	104	23	W
PSALM	103	4	B	PSALM	103	21	W	PSALM	104	24	D
PSALM	103	4	W	PSALM	103	22	B	PSALM	104	24	W
PSALM	103	5	B	PSALM	103	22	W	PSALM	104	25	D
PSALM	103	5	W	PSALM	104	1	D	PSALM	104	25	W
PSALM	103	6	B	PSALM	104	1	W	PSALM	104	26	D
PSALM	103	6	D	PSALM	104	2	D	PSALM	104	26	W
PSALM	103	6	W	PSALM	104	2	W	PSALM	104	27	D
PSALM	103	7	B	PSALM	104	3	D	PSALM	104	27	W
PSALM	103	7	TSR	PSALM	104	3	W	PSALM	104	28	D
PSALM	103	7	W	PSALM	104	4	D	PSALM	104	28	W
PSALM	103	8	B	PSALM	104	4	W	PSALM	104	29	D
PSALM	103	8	D	PSALM	104	5	D	PSALM	104	29	W
PSALM	103	8	W	PSALM	104	5	W	PSALM	104	30	D
PSALM	103	9	B	PSALM	104	6	D	PSALM	104	30	W
PSALM	103	9	D	PSALM	104	6	W	PSALM	104	31	D
PSALM	103	9	W	PSALM	104	7	D	PSALM	104	31	W
PSALM	103	10	B	PSALM	104	7	W	PSALM	104	32	D
PSALM	103	10	D	PSALM	104	8	D	PSALM	104	32	W
PSALM	103	10	W	PSALM	104	8	W	PSALM	104	33	D
PSALM	103	11·	B	PSALM	104	9	D	PSALM	104	33	W
PSALM	103	11	D	PSALM	104	9	W	PSALM	104	34	D
PSALM	103	11	W	PSALM	104	10	D	PSALM	104	34	W
PSALM	103	12	B	PSALM	104	10	W	PSALM	104	35	D
PSALM	103	12	D	PSALM	104	11	D	PSALM	104	35	W
PSALM	103	12	W	PSALM	104	11	W	PSALM	105	1	W
PSALM	103	13	B	PSALM	104	12	D	PSALM	105	2	W
PSALM	103	13	D	PSALM	104	12	W	PSALM	105	3	W
PSALM	103	13	W	PSALM	104	13	D	PSALM	105	4	D
PSALM	103	14	B	PSALM	104	13	W	PSALM	105	5	TSR
PSALM	103	14	D	PSALM	104	14	D	PSALM	105	6	TSR
PSALM	103	14	W	PSALM	104	14	W	PSALM	105	7	D
PSALM	103	15	B	PSALM	104	15	D	PSALM	105	8	TSR
PSALM	103	15	D	PSALM	104	15	W	PSALM	105	9	TSR
PSALM	103	15	W	PSALM	104	16	D	PSALM	105	10	TSR
PSALM	103	16	B	PSALM	104	16	W	PSALM	105	11	TSR
PSALM	103	16	D	PSALM	104	17	D	PSALM	105	12	TSR
PSALM	103	16	W	PSALM	104	17	W	PSALM	105	13	TSR
PSALM	103	17	B	PSALM	104	18	D	PSALM	105	14	TSR
PSALM	103	17	D	PSALM	104	18	W	PSALM	105	15	TSR
PSALM	103	17	W	PSALM	104	19	D	PSALM	105	16	TSR
PSALM	103	18	B	PSALM	104	19	W	PSALM	105	17	TSR

P.1 Prosperity P.2 Peace P.3 Health P.4 Spread Gospel P.5 Fill Promises P.6 Save from Enemies P.7 Hear my Prayer B – Blessing D - Doctrine C - Confession TSR – Salvation G – Groaning W – Worship M – Messianic R – Rebuke S – Science

PSALM				PSALM				PSALM			
PSALM	105	18	TSR	PSALM	106	22	TSR	PSALM	107	23	TSR
PSALM	105	19	TSR	PSALM	106	23	TSR	PSALM	107	24	TSR
PSALM	105	20	TSR	PSALM	106	24	TSR	PSALM	107	25	TSR
PSALM	105	21	TSR	PSALM	106	25	TSR	PSALM	107	26	TSR
PSALM	105	22	TSR	PSALM	106	26	TSR	PSALM	107	27	TSR
PSALM	105	23	TSR	PSALM	106	27	TSR	PSALM	107	28	TSR
PSALM	105	24	TSR	PSALM	106	28	TSR	PSALM	107	29	TSR
PSALM	105	25	TSR	PSALM	106	29	TSR	PSALM	107	30	TSR
PSALM	105	26	TSR	PSALM	106	30	TSR	PSALM	107	31	G
PSALM	105	27	TSR	PSALM	106	31	TSR	PSALM	107	32	D
PSALM	105	28	TSR	PSALM	106	32	TSR	PSALM	107	33	D
PSALM	105	29	TSR	PSALM	106	33	TSR	PSALM	107	34	D
PSALM	105	30	TSR	PSALM	106	34	TSR	PSALM	107	35	D
PSALM	105	31	TSR	PSALM	106	35	TSR	PSALM	107	36	D
PSALM	105	32	TSR	PSALM	106	36	TSR	PSALM	107	37	D
PSALM	105	33	TSR	PSALM	106	37	TSR	PSALM	107	38	D
PSALM	105	34	TSR	PSALM	106	38	TSR	PSALM	107	39	D
PSALM	105	35	TSR	PSALM	106	39	TSR	PSALM	107	40	D
PSALM	105	36	TSR	PSALM	106	40	TSR	PSALM	107	41	D
PSALM	105	37	TSR	PSALM	106	41	TSR	PSALM	107	42	D
PSALM	105	38	TSR	PSALM	106	42	TSR	PSALM	107	43	D
PSALM	105	39	TSR	PSALM	106	43	TSR	PSALM	108	1	W
PSALM	105	40	TSR	PSALM	106	44	TSR	PSALM	108	2	W
PSALM	105	41	TSR	PSALM	106	45	TSR	PSALM	108	3	W
PSALM	105	42	TSR	PSALM	106	46	TSR	PSALM	108	4	W
PSALM	105	43	TSR	PSALM	106	47	P.1	PSALM	108	5	P.4
PSALM	105	44	TSR	PSALM	106	48	W	PSALM	108	6	P.2
PSALM	105	45	TSR	PSALM	107	1	W	PSALM	108	7	D
PSALM	106	1	W	PSALM	107	2	D	PSALM	108	8	D
PSALM	106	2	W	PSALM	107	3	D	PSALM	108	9	D
PSALM	106	3	B	PSALM	107	4	TSR	PSALM	108	10	W
PSALM	106	4	P.1	PSALM	107	5	TSR	PSALM	108	11	W
PSALM	106	5	P.1	PSALM	107	6	TSR	PSALM	108	12	P.2
PSALM	106	6	C	PSALM	107	7	TSR	PSALM	108	13	D
PSALM	106	7	TSR	PSALM	107	8	G	PSALM	109	1	P.6
PSALM	106	8	TSR	PSALM	107	9	D	PSALM	109	2	P.6
PSALM	106	9	TSR	PSALM	107	10	R	PSALM	109	3	P.6
PSALM	106	10	TSR	PSALM	107	11	R	PSALM	109	4	P.6
PSALM	106	11	TSR	PSALM	107	12	R	PSALM	109	5	P.6
PSALM	106	12	TSR	PSALM	107	13	TSR	PSALM	109	6	M
PSALM	106	13	TSR	PSALM	107	14	TSR	PSALM	109	7	M
PSALM	106	14	TSR	PSALM	107	15	G	PSALM	109	8	M
PSALM	106	15	TSR	PSALM	107	16	TSR	PSALM	109	9	P.5
PSALM	106	16	TSR	PSALM	107	17	TSR	PSALM	109	10	P.5
PSALM	106	17	TSR	PSALM	107	18	TSR	PSALM	109	11	P.5
PSALM	106	18	TSR	PSALM	107	19	TSR	PSALM	109	12	P.5
PSALM	106	19	TSR	PSALM	107	20	TSR	PSALM	109	13	P.5
PSALM	106	20	TSR	PSALM	107	21	G	PSALM	109	14	P.5
PSALM	106	21	TSR	PSALM	107	22	D	PSALM	109	15	P.5

P.1 Prosperity P.2 Peace P.3 Health P.4 Spread Gospel P.5 Fill Promises P.6 Save from Enemies P.7 Hear my Prayer B – Blessing D - Doctrine C - Confession TSR – Salvation G – Groaning W – Worship M – Messianic R – Rebuke S – Science

Psalms Categories by Chapter and Verse

PSALM	109	16	P.5	PSALM	113	6	W	PSALM	116	17	TSR
PSALM	109	17	P.5	PSALM	113	7	HANNA'S PRAYER	PSALM	116	18	TSR
PSALM	109	18	P.5	PSALM	113	7	W	PSALM	116	19	TSR
PSALM	109	19	P.5	PSALM	113	8	HANNA'S PRAYER	PSALM	117	1	W
PSALM	109	20	P.5	PSALM	113	8	W	PSALM	117	2	W
PSALM	109	21	P.1	PSALM	113	9	W	PSALM	118	1	W
PSALM	109	22	P.1	PSALM	114	1	TSR	PSALM	118	2	W
PSALM	109	23	P.1	PSALM	114	2	TSR	PSALM	118	3	W
PSALM	109	24	P.1	PSALM	114	3	TSR	PSALM	118	4	W
PSALM	109	25	M	PSALM	114	4	TSR	PSALM	118	5	TSR
PSALM	109	26	M	PSALM	114	5	TSR	PSALM	118	6	TSR
PSALM	109	27	M	PSALM	114	6	TSR	PSALM	118	7	D
PSALM	109	28	P.1	PSALM	114	7	D	PSALM	118	8	D
PSALM	109	29	P.5	PSALM	114	8	D	PSALM	118	9	D
PSALM	109	30	W	PSALM	115	1	P.4	PSALM	118	10	TSR
PSALM	109	31	W	PSALM	115	2	P.4	PSALM	118	11	TSR
PSALM	110	1	M	PSALM	115	3	D	PSALM	118	12	TSR
PSALM	110	2	D	PSALM	115	4	D	PSALM	118	13	TSR
PSALM	110	3	D	PSALM	115	5	D	PSALM	118	14	D
PSALM	110	4	D	PSALM	115	6	D	PSALM	118	15	D
PSALM	110	5	D	PSALM	115	7	D	PSALM	118	16	D
PSALM	110	6	D	PSALM	115	8	D	PSALM	118	17	D
PSALM	110	7	D	PSALM	115	9	D	PSALM	118	18	G
PSALM	111	1	W	PSALM	115	10	D	PSALM	118	19	W
PSALM	111	2	W	PSALM	115	11	D	PSALM	118	20	W
PSALM	111	3	W	PSALM	115	12	D	PSALM	118	21	W
PSALM	111	4	TSR	PSALM	115	13	D	PSALM	118	22	M
PSALM	111	5	TSR	PSALM	115	14	D	PSALM	118	23	M
PSALM	111	6	TSR	PSALM	115	15	D	PSALM	118	24	M
PSALM	111	7	W	PSALM	115	16	D	PSALM	118	25	P.1
PSALM	111	8	D	PSALM	115	17	W	PSALM	118	26	W
PSALM	111	9	TSR	PSALM	115	18	W	PSALM	118	27	W
PSALM	111	10	D	PSALM	116	1	TSR	PSALM	118	28	W
PSALM	112	1	W	PSALM	116	2	TSR	PSALM	118	29	W
PSALM	112	2	D	PSALM	116	3	TSR	PSALM	119	1	B
PSALM	112	3	D	PSALM	116	4	TSR	PSALM	119	1	W
PSALM	112	4	D	PSALM	116	5	TSR	PSALM	119	2	B
PSALM	112	5	D	PSALM	116	6	TSR	PSALM	119	2	W
PSALM	112	6	D	PSALM	116	7	TSR	PSALM	119	3	B
PSALM	112	7	D	PSALM	116	8	TSR	PSALM	119	3	W
PSALM	112	8	D	PSALM	116	9	TSR	PSALM	119	4	D
PSALM	112	9	D	PSALM	116	10	TSR	PSALM	119	5	G
PSALM	112	10	D	PSALM	116	11	TSR	PSALM	119	6	G
PSALM	113	1	W	PSALM	116	12	TSR	PSALM	119	7	G
PSALM	113	2	W	PSALM	116	13	TSR	PSALM	119	8	G
PSALM	113	3	W	PSALM	116	14	TSR	PSALM	119	9	P.3
PSALM	113	4	D	PSALM	116	15	D	PSALM	119	9	W
PSALM	113	4	W	PSALM	116	15	TSR	PSALM	119	10	P.2
PSALM	113	5	W	PSALM	116	16	TSR	PSALM	119	11	P.2

P.1 Prosperity P.2 Peace P.3 Health P.4 Spread Gospel P.5 Fill Promises P.6 Save from Enemies
P.7 Hear my Prayer B – Blessing D - Doctrine C - Confession TSR – Salvation G – Groaning W –
Worship M – Messianic R – Rebuke S – Science

PSALM	119	11	W	PSALM	119	57	W	PSALM	119	103	W
PSALM	119	12	P.7	PSALM	119	58	W	PSALM	119	104	W
PSALM	119	12	W	PSALM	119	59	W	PSALM	119	105	W
PSALM	119	13	W	PSALM	119	60	W	PSALM	119	106	W
PSALM	119	14	W	PSALM	119	61	W	PSALM	119	107	P.1
PSALM	119	15	W	PSALM	119	62	W	PSALM	119	108	P.7
PSALM	119	16	W	PSALM	119	63	W	PSALM	119	109	W
PSALM	119	17	P.1	PSALM	119	64	W	PSALM	119	110	W
PSALM	119	18	P.7	PSALM	119	65	W	PSALM	119	111	W
PSALM	119	19	P.7	PSALM	119	66	P.7	PSALM	119	112	W
PSALM	119	20	W	PSALM	119	67	W	PSALM	119	113	W
PSALM	119	21	P.2	PSALM	119	68	P.7	PSALM	119	114	W
PSALM	119	22	P.2	PSALM	119	69	W	PSALM	119	115	W
PSALM	119	23	W	PSALM	119	70	W	PSALM	119	116	P.2
PSALM	119	24	W	PSALM	119	71	W	PSALM	119	117	P.2
PSALM	119	25	G	PSALM	119	72	W	PSALM	119	118	W
PSALM	119	26	P.7	PSALM	119	73	P.7	PSALM	119	119	W
PSALM	119	27	P.7	PSALM	119	73	W	PSALM	119	120	W
PSALM	119	28	G	PSALM	119	74	W	PSALM	119	121	P.6
PSALM	119	29	P.3	PSALM	119	75	W	PSALM	119	122	P.6
PSALM	119	30	W	PSALM	119	76	P.2	PSALM	119	123	W
PSALM	119	31	P.2	PSALM	119	77	P.3	PSALM	119	124	P.7
PSALM	119	31	W	PSALM	119	78	P.6	PSALM	119	125	P.7
PSALM	119	32	W	PSALM	119	79	P.4	PSALM	119	126	W
PSALM	119	33	P.7	PSALM	119	80	P.2	PSALM	119	127	W
PSALM	119	34	P.7	PSALM	119	81	P.2	PSALM	119	128	W
PSALM	119	35	P.4	PSALM	119	81	W	PSALM	119	129	W
PSALM	119	36	P.3	PSALM	119	82	W	PSALM	119	130	W
PSALM	119	37	P.3	PSALM	119	83	W	PSALM	119	131	W
PSALM	119	38	P.1	PSALM	119	84	P.6	PSALM	119	132	P.2
PSALM	119	39	P.6	PSALM	119	84	W	PSALM	119	133	P.3
PSALM	119	40	P.1	PSALM	119	85	P.6	PSALM	119	134	P.6
PSALM	119	41	P.1	PSALM	119	86	P.6	PSALM	119	135	P.7
PSALM	119	42	P.2	PSALM	119	87	P.6	PSALM	119	136	W
PSALM	119	43	P.3	PSALM	119	88	P.1	PSALM	119	137	W
PSALM	119	44	W	PSALM	119	89	W	PSALM	119	138	W
PSALM	119	45	W	PSALM	119	90	W	PSALM	119	139	W
PSALM	119	46	P.4	PSALM	119	91	W	PSALM	119	140	W
PSALM	119	46	W	PSALM	119	92	W	PSALM	119	141	W
PSALM	119	47	W	PSALM	119	93	W	PSALM	119	142	W
PSALM	119	48	W	PSALM	119	94	P.6	PSALM	119	143	W
PSALM	119	49	P.2	PSALM	119	95	W	PSALM	119	144	P.7
PSALM	119	50	W	PSALM	119	96	W	PSALM	119	145	W
PSALM	119	51	W	PSALM	119	97	W	PSALM	119	146	W
PSALM	119	52	W	PSALM	119	98	W	PSALM	119	147	W
PSALM	119	53	W	PSALM	119	99	W	PSALM	119	148	W
PSALM	119	54	W	PSALM	119	100	W	PSALM	119	149	P.1
PSALM	119	55	W	PSALM	119	101	W	PSALM	119	150	W
PSALM	119	56	W	PSALM	119	102	W	PSALM	119	151	W

P.1 Prosperity P.2 Peace P.3 Health P.4 Spread Gospel P.5 Fill Promises P.6 Save from Enemies P.7 Hear my Prayer B – Blessing D - Doctrine C - Confession TSR – Salvation G – Groaning W – Worship M – Messianic R – Rebuke S – Science

Psalms Categories by Chapter and Verse

PSALM	119	152	W	PSALM	122	7	W	PSALM	130	1	G
PSALM	119	153	P.2	PSALM	122	8	P.1	PSALM	130	2	G
PSALM	119	154	P.6	PSALM	122	8	W	PSALM	130	3	P.3
PSALM	119	155	W	PSALM	122	9	W	PSALM	130	3	W
PSALM	119	156	P.1	PSALM	123	1	P.2	PSALM	130	4	P.2
PSALM	119	156	W	PSALM	123	1	W	PSALM	130	4	W
PSALM	119	157	W	PSALM	123	2	P.2	PSALM	130	5	W
PSALM	119	158	W	PSALM	123	2	W	PSALM	130	6	W
PSALM	119	159	P.1	PSALM	123	3	P.2	PSALM	130	7	W
PSALM	119	160	W	PSALM	123	3	W	PSALM	130	8	W
PSALM	119	161	W	PSALM	123	4	G	PSALM	131	1	P.2
PSALM	119	162	W	PSALM	124	1	TSR	PSALM	131	1	W
PSALM	119	163	W	PSALM	124	2	TSR	PSALM	131	2	P.2
PSALM	119	164	W	PSALM	124	3	TSR	PSALM	131	2	W
PSALM	119	165	W	PSALM	124	4	TSR	PSALM	131	3	W
PSALM	119	166	W	PSALM	124	5	TSR	PSALM	132	1	P.1
PSALM	119	167	W	PSALM	124	6	TSR	PSALM	132	1	W
PSALM	119	168	W	PSALM	124	7	TSR	PSALM	132	2	P.1
PSALM	119	169	P.2	PSALM	124	8	TSR	PSALM	132	2	W
PSALM	119	170	P.2	PSALM	125	1	W	PSALM	132	3	W
PSALM	119	171	W	PSALM	125	2	W	PSALM	132	4	W
PSALM	119	172	W	PSALM	125	3	W	PSALM	132	5	W
PSALM	119	173	P.2	PSALM	125	4	P.1	PSALM	132	6	W
PSALM	119	174	P.1	PSALM	125	5	P.1	PSALM	132	7	W
PSALM	119	174	W	PSALM	126	1	W	PSALM	132	8	P.4
PSALM	119	175	P.1	PSALM	126	2	W	PSALM	132	8	W
PSALM	119	176	P.3	PSALM	126	3	W	PSALM	132	9	P.4
PSALM	120	1	G	PSALM	126	4	P.2	PSALM	132	9	W
PSALM	120	2	P.6	PSALM	126	5	W	PSALM	132	10	P.4
PSALM	120	3	R	PSALM	126	6	W	PSALM	132	10	W
PSALM	120	4	R	PSALM	127	1	D	PSALM	132	11	D
PSALM	120	5	R	PSALM	127	2	D	PSALM	132	11	M
PSALM	120	6	R	PSALM	127	3	D	PSALM	132	12	D
PSALM	120	7	R	PSALM	127	4	D	PSALM	132	12	M
PSALM	121	1	W	PSALM	127	5	D	PSALM	132	13	D
PSALM	121	2	W	PSALM	128	1	D	PSALM	132	13	M
PSALM	121	3	W	PSALM	128	2	D	PSALM	132	14	D
PSALM	121	4	W	PSALM	128	3	D	PSALM	132	14	M
PSALM	121	5	W	PSALM	128	4	D	PSALM	132	15	D
PSALM	121	6	W	PSALM	128	5	D	PSALM	132	15	M
PSALM	121	7	W	PSALM	128	6	D	PSALM	132	16	D
PSALM	121	8	W	PSALM	129	1	G	PSALM	132	16	M
PSALM	122	1	W	PSALM	129	2	G	PSALM	132	17	D
PSALM	122	2	W	PSALM	129	3	G	PSALM	132	17	M
PSALM	122	3	W	PSALM	129	4	G	PSALM	132	18	D
PSALM	122	4	W	PSALM	129	5	P.6	PSALM	132	18	M
PSALM	122	5	W	PSALM	129	6	P.6	PSALM	133	1	W
PSALM	122	6	P.1	PSALM	129	7	P.6	PSALM	133	2	W
PSALM	122	7	P.1	PSALM	129	8	P.6	PSALM	133	3	W

P.1 Prosperity P.2 Peace P.3 Health P.4 Spread Gospel P.5 Fill Promises P.6 Save from Enemies
P.7 Hear my Prayer B – Blessing D - Doctrine C - Confession TSR – Salvation G – Groaning W –
Worship M – Messianic R – Rebuke S – Science

PSALM				PSALM				PSALM			
PSALM	134	1	W	PSALM	136	25	S	PSALM	140	6	P.7
PSALM	134	2	W	PSALM	136	26	W	PSALM	140	7	TSR
PSALM	134	3	W	PSALM	137	1	W	PSALM	140	8	P.6
PSALM	135	1	W	PSALM	137	2	W	PSALM	140	9	P.6
PSALM	135	2	W	PSALM	137	3	W	PSALM	140	10	P.5
PSALM	135	3	W	PSALM	137	4	W	PSALM	140	11	P.5
PSALM	135	4	W	PSALM	137	5	W	PSALM	140	12	P.5
PSALM	135	5	W	PSALM	137	6	W	PSALM	140	12	P.5
PSALM	135	6	W	PSALM	137	7	P.5	PSALM	140	13	P.5
PSALM	135	7	S	PSALM	137	8	P.5	PSALM	141	1	P.7
PSALM	135	7	W	PSALM	137	9	P.5	PSALM	141	2	P.7
PSALM	135	8	W	PSALM	138	1	W	PSALM	141	3	P.3
PSALM	135	9	W	PSALM	138	2	W	PSALM	141	4	P.3
PSALM	135	10	W	PSALM	138	3	W	PSALM	141	5	P.3
PSALM	135	11	W	PSALM	138	4	W	PSALM	141	6	G
PSALM	135	12	W	PSALM	138	5	W	PSALM	141	7	G
PSALM	135	13	W	PSALM	138	6	W	PSALM	141	8	G
PSALM	135	14	W	PSALM	138	7	W	PSALM	141	9	G
PSALM	135	15	W	PSALM	138	8	P.1	PSALM	141	10	G
PSALM	135	16	W	PSALM	138	8	W	PSALM	142	1	G
PSALM	135	17	W	PSALM	139	1	W	PSALM	142	2	G
PSALM	135	18	W	PSALM	139	2	W	PSALM	142	3	G
PSALM	135	19	W	PSALM	139	3	W	PSALM	142	4	G
PSALM	135	20	W	PSALM	139	4	W	PSALM	142	5	G
PSALM	135	21	W	PSALM	139	5	W	PSALM	142	6	G
PSALM	136	1	W	PSALM	139	6	W	PSALM	142	7	G
PSALM	136	2	W	PSALM	139	7	W	PSALM	143	2	C
PSALM	136	3	W	PSALM	139	8	W	PSALM	143	3	G
PSALM	136	4	W	PSALM	139	9	W	PSALM	143	4	G
PSALM	136	5	S	PSALM	139	10	W	PSALM	143	5	G
PSALM	136	6	S	PSALM	139	11	W	PSALM	143	6	G
PSALM	136	7	S	PSALM	139	12	W	PSALM	143	7	G
PSALM	136	8	S	PSALM	139	13	W	PSALM	143	8	G
PSALM	136	9	S	PSALM	139	14	W	PSALM	143	9	G
PSALM	136	10	W	PSALM	139	15	W	PSALM	143	10	G
PSALM	136	11	W	PSALM	139	16	W	PSALM	143	11	G
PSALM	136	12	W	PSALM	139	17	W	PSALM	143	12	G
PSALM	136	13	S	PSALM	139	18	W	PSALM	144	1	PZW
PSALM	136	14	S	PSALM	139	19	W	PSALM	144	2	PZW
PSALM	136	15	S	PSALM	139	20	G	PSALM	144	3	P.5
PSALM	136	16	S	PSALM	139	21	G	PSALM	144	4	P.5
PSALM	136	17	W	PSALM	139	22	G	PSALM	144	5	P.5
PSALM	136	18	W	PSALM	139	23	C	PSALM	144	6	P.6
PSALM	136	19	W	PSALM	139	24	C	PSALM	144	7	P.6
PSALM	136	20	W	PSALM	140	1	P.6	PSALM	144	8	P.6
PSALM	136	21	W	PSALM	140	2	P.6	PSALM	144	9	PZW
PSALM	136	22	W	PSALM	140	3	P.6	PSALM	144	10	PZW
PSALM	136	23	W	PSALM	140	4	P.6	PSALM	144	11	P.7
PSALM	136	24	W	PSALM	140	5	P.6	PSALM	144	12	P.7

P.1 Prosperity P.2 Peace P.3 Health P.4 Spread Gospel P.5 Fill Promises P.6 Save from Enemies P.7 Hear my Prayer B – Blessing D - Doctrine C - Confession TSR – Salvation G – Groaning W – Worship M – Messianic R – Rebuke S – Science

PSALM	144	13	P.7	PSALM	147	15	PZW				
PSALM	144	14	P.7	PSALM	147	16	S				
PSALM	144	15	PZW	PSALM	147	17	S				
PSALM	145	1	PZW	PSALM	147	18	S				
PSALM	145	2	PZW	PSALM	147	19	PZW				
PSALM	145	3	PZW	PSALM	147	20	PZW				
PSALM	145	4	PZW	PSALM	148	1	PZW				
PSALM	145	5	PZW	PSALM	148	2	PZW				
PSALM	145	6	PZW	PSALM	148	3	PZW				
PSALM	145	7	PZW	PSALM	148	4	PZW				
PSALM	145	8	PZW	PSALM	148	5	PZW				
PSALM	145	9	PZW	PSALM	148	6	PZW				
PSALM	145	10	PZW	PSALM	148	7	PZW				
PSALM	145	11	PZW	PSALM	148	8	PZW				
PSALM	145	12	PZW	PSALM	148	9	PZW				
PSALM	145	13	PZW	PSALM	148	10	PZW				
PSALM	145	14	PZW	PSALM	148	11	PZW				
PSALM	145	15	PZW	PSALM	148	12	PZW				
PSALM	145	16	PZW	PSALM	148	13	PZW				
PSALM	145	17	PZW	PSALM	148	14	PZW				
PSALM	145	18	PZW	PSALM	149	1	PZW				
PSALM	145	19	PZW	PSALM	149	2	PZW				
PSALM	145	20	PZW	PSALM	149	3	PZW				
PSALM	145	21	PZW	PSALM	149	4	PZW				
PSALM	146	1	PZW	PSALM	149	5	PZW				
PSALM	146	2	PZW	PSALM	149	6	PZW				
PSALM	146	3	PZW	PSALM	149	7	PZW				
PSALM	146	4	PZW	PSALM	149	8	PZW				
PSALM	146	5	PZW	PSALM	149	9	PZW				
PSALM	146	6	PZW	PSALM	150	1	PZW				
PSALM	146	7	PZW	PSALM	150	2	PZW				
PSALM	146	8	PZW	PSALM	150	3	PZW				
PSALM	146	9	PZW	PSALM	150	4	PZW				
PSALM	146	10	PZW	PSALM	150	5	PZW				
PSALM	147	1	PZW	PSALM	150	6	PZW				
PSALM	147	2	PZW								
PSALM	147	3	PZW								
PSALM	147	4	PZW								
PSALM	147	4	S								
PSALM	147	5	PZW								
PSALM	147	6	PZW								
PSALM	147	7	PZW								
PSALM	147	8	S								
PSALM	147	9	PZW								
PSALM	147	10	PZW								
PSALM	147	11	PZW								
PSALM	147	12	PZW								
PSALM	147	13	PZW								
PSALM	147	14	PZW								

P.1 Prosperity P.2 Peace P.3 Health P.4 Spread Gospel P.5 Fill Promises P.6 Save from Enemies
P.7 Hear my Prayer B – Blessing D - Doctrine C - Confession TSR – Salvation G – Groaning W –
Worship M – Messianic R – Rebuke S – Science

Categories

This section is divided into the smaller categories. This will allow one to search for a particular type of verse. If one wants to pray for a confession, simply go to the Confession section on page 27.

Blessing

PSALM	1	1	B
PSALM	1	2	B
PSALM	1	3	B
PSALM	1	4	B
PSALM	1	5	B
PSALM	1	6	B
PSALM	2	12	B
PSALM	20	1	B
PSALM	20	2	B
PSALM	20	3	B
PSALM	20	4	B
PSALM	41	1	B
PSALM	41	2	B
PSALM	41	3	B
PSALM	65	4	B
PSALM	89	15	B
PSALM	103	1	B
PSALM	103	2	B
PSALM	103	3	B
PSALM	103	4	B
PSALM	103	5	B
PSALM	103	6	B
PSALM	103	7	B
PSALM	103	8	B
PSALM	103	9	B
PSALM	103	10	B
PSALM	103	11	B
PSALM	103	12	B
PSALM	103	13	B
PSALM	103	14	B
PSALM	103	15	B
PSALM	103	16	B
PSALM	103	17	B
PSALM	103	18	B
PSALM	103	19	B
PSALM	103	20	B
PSALM	103	21	B
PSALM	103	22	B
PSALM	106	3	B
PSALM	119	1	B
PSALM	119	2	B
PSALM	119	3	B

Confession - Make Clear

PSALM	6	2	C
PSALM	19	12	C
PSALM	25	7	C
PSALM	25	11	C
PSALM	25	18	C
PSALM	26	2	C
PSALM	32	5	C
PSALM	38	1	C
PSALM	38	2	C
PSALM	38	3	C
PSALM	38	4	C
PSALM	38	5	C
PSALM	38	6	C
PSALM	38	7	C
PSALM	38	8	C
PSALM	38	18	C
PSALM	39	8	C
PSALM	41	4	C
PSALM	51	3	C
PSALM	51	9	C
PSALM	51	10	C
PSALM	51	11	C
PSALM	51	12	C
PSALM	51	14	C
PSALM	62	5	C
PSALM	65	3	C
PSALM	69	5	C
PSALM	79	8	C
PSALM	79	9	C
PSALM	101	3	C
PSALM	101	4	C
PSALM	101	5	C
PSALM	106	6	C
PSALM	139	23	C
PSALM	139	24	C
PSALM	143	2	C

PSALM	3	8	D	PSALM	14	1	D	PSALM	28	5	D
PSALM	4	3	D	PSALM	14	2	D	PSALM	29	1	D
PSALM	4	4	D	PSALM	14	3	D	PSALM	29	2	D
PSALM	4	5	D	PSALM	14	4	D	PSALM	29	3	D
PSALM	4	6	D	PSALM	14	4	D	PSALM	29	4	D
PSALM	7	10	D	PSALM	15	2	D	PSALM	29	5	D
PSALM	7	11	D	PSALM	15	3	D	PSALM	29	6	D
PSALM	7	12	D	PSALM	15	4	D	PSALM	29	7	D
PSALM	7	13	D	PSALM	15	5	D	PSALM	29	8	D
PSALM	7	14	D	PSALM	18	7	D	PSALM	29	9	D
PSALM	7	15	D	PSALM	18	8	D	PSALM	29	10	D
PSALM	7	16	D	PSALM	18	9	D	PSALM	29	11	D
PSALM	7	17	D	PSALM	18	10	D	PSALM	30	5	D
PSALM	8	1	D	PSALM	18	11	D	PSALM	31	23	D
PSALM	8	4	D	PSALM	18	12	D	PSALM	31	24	D
PSALM	8	5	D	PSALM	18	13	D	PSALM	32	8	D
PSALM	8	6	D	PSALM	18	14	D	PSALM	32	9	D
PSALM	8	7	D	PSALM	18	15	D	PSALM	32	10	D
PSALM	9	7	D	PSALM	18	30	D	PSALM	32	11	D
PSALM	9	8	D	PSALM	18	31	D	PSALM	33	1	D
PSALM	9	9	D	PSALM	18	32	D	PSALM	33	2	D
PSALM	9	11	D	PSALM	18	33	D	PSALM	33	3	D
PSALM	9	12	D	PSALM	18	34	D	PSALM	33	4	D
PSALM	9	15	D	PSALM	18	41	D	PSALM	33	5	D
PSALM	9	16	D	PSALM	19	7	D	PSALM	33	6	D
PSALM	9	17	D	PSALM	19	8	D	PSALM	33	7	D
PSALM	9	18	D	PSALM	19	9	D	PSALM	33	8	D
PSALM	10	2	D	PSALM	19	10	D	PSALM	33	9	D
PSALM	10	3	D	PSALM	19	11	D	PSALM	33	10	D
PSALM	10	4	D	PSALM	20	6	D	PSALM	33	11	D
PSALM	10	6	D	PSALM	22	23	D	PSALM	33	12	D
PSALM	10	7	D	PSALM	22	26	D	PSALM	33	13	D
PSALM	10	8	D	PSALM	22	27	D	PSALM	33	14	D
PSALM	10	9	D	PSALM	22	28	D	PSALM	33	15	D
PSALM	10	10	D	PSALM	22	29	D	PSALM	33	16	D
PSALM	10	11	D	PSALM	22	30	D	PSALM	33	17	D
PSALM	10	13	D	PSALM	22	31	D	PSALM	33	18	D
PSALM	10	16	D	PSALM	24	3	D	PSALM	33	19	D
PSALM	11	2	D	PSALM	24	4	D	PSALM	34	3	D
PSALM	11	4	D	PSALM	24	5	D	PSALM	34	7	D
PSALM	11	5	D	PSALM	24	6	D	PSALM	34	8	D
PSALM	11	6	D	PSALM	24	10	D	PSALM	34	9	D
PSALM	11	7	D	PSALM	25	8	D	PSALM	34	10	D
PSALM	12	3	D	PSALM	25	9	D	PSALM	34	11	D
PSALM	12	4	D	PSALM	25	10	D	PSALM	34	12	D
PSALM	12	5	D	PSALM	25	12	D	PSALM	34	13	D
PSALM	12	6	D	PSALM	25	13	D	PSALM	34	14	D
PSALM	12	8	D	PSALM	25	14	D	PSALM	34	15	D
PSALM	13	6	D	PSALM	27	14	D	PSALM	34	16	D

PSALM	34	17	D	PSALM	37	34	D	PSALM	48	13	D
PSALM	34	18	D	PSALM	37	35	D	PSALM	48	14	D
PSALM	34	19	D	PSALM	37	36	D	PSALM	49	1	D
PSALM	34	20	D	PSALM	37	37	D	PSALM	49	2	D
PSALM	34	21	D	PSALM	37	38	D	PSALM	49	3	D
PSALM	34	22	D	PSALM	37	39	D	PSALM	49	4	D
PSALM	36	1	D	PSALM	37	40	D	PSALM	49	5	D
PSALM	36	2	D	PSALM	39	6	D	PSALM	49	6	D
PSALM	36	3	D	PSALM	44	21	D	PSALM	49	7	D
PSALM	36	4	D	PSALM	44	22	D	PSALM	49	8	D
PSALM	36	5	D	PSALM	45	6	D	PSALM	49	9	D
PSALM	36	6	D	PSALM	45	9	D	PSALM	49	10	D
PSALM	36	7	D	PSALM	45	10	D	PSALM	49	11	D
PSALM	36	8	D	PSALM	45	11	D	PSALM	49	12	D
PSALM	36	9	D	PSALM	45	12	D	PSALM	49	13	D
PSALM	36	12	D	PSALM	45	13	D	PSALM	49	14	D
PSALM	37	1	D	PSALM	45	14	D	PSALM	49	15	D
PSALM	37	2	D	PSALM	45	15	D	PSALM	49	16	D
PSALM	37	3	D	PSALM	45	16	D	PSALM	49	17	D
PSALM	37	4	D	PSALM	45	17	D	PSALM	49	18	D
PSALM	37	5	D	PSALM	46	1	D	PSALM	49	19	D
PSALM	37	6	D	PSALM	46	2	D	PSALM	49	20	D
PSALM	37	7	D	PSALM	46	3	D	PSALM	50	1	D
PSALM	37	8	D	PSALM	46	4	D	PSALM	50	2	D
PSALM	37	9	D	PSALM	46	5	D	PSALM	50	3	D
PSALM	37	10	D	PSALM	46	6	D	PSALM	50	4	D
PSALM	37	11	D	PSALM	46	7	D	PSALM	50	5	D
PSALM	37	12	D	PSALM	46	8	D	PSALM	50	6	D
PSALM	37	13	D	PSALM	46	9	D	PSALM	50	7	D
PSALM	37	14	D	PSALM	46	10	D	PSALM	50	8	D
PSALM	37	15	D	PSALM	46	11	D	PSALM	50	9	D
PSALM	37	16	D	PSALM	47	1	D	PSALM	50	10	D
PSALM	37	17	D	PSALM	47	2	D	PSALM	50	11	D
PSALM	37	18	D	PSALM	47	3	D	PSALM	50	12	D
PSALM	37	19	D	PSALM	47	4	D	PSALM	50	13	D
PSALM	37	20	D	PSALM	47	5	D	PSALM	50	14	D
PSALM	37	21	D	PSALM	47	6	D	PSALM	50	15	D
PSALM	37	22	D	PSALM	47	7	D	PSALM	50	16	D
PSALM	37	23	D	PSALM	47	8	D	PSALM	50	17	D
PSALM	37	24	D	PSALM	47	9	D	PSALM	50	18	D
PSALM	37	25	D	PSALM	48	1	D	PSALM	50	19	D
PSALM	37	26	D	PSALM	48	2	D	PSALM	50	20	D
PSALM	37	27	D	PSALM	48	3	D	PSALM	50	21	D
PSALM	37	28	D	PSALM	48	4	D	PSALM	50	22	D
PSALM	37	29	D	PSALM	48	5	D	PSALM	50	23	D
PSALM	37	30	D	PSALM	48	6	D	PSALM	51	4	D
PSALM	37	31	D	PSALM	48	7	D	PSALM	51	5	D
PSALM	37	32	D	PSALM	48	8	D	PSALM	51	6	D
PSALM	37	33	D	PSALM	48	12	D	PSALM	51	19	D

PSALM	52	6	D	PSALM	68	20	D	PSALM	75	7	D
PSALM	52	7	D	PSALM	68	21	D	PSALM	76	1	D
PSALM	52	8	D	PSALM	68	22	D	PSALM	76	2	D
PSALM	53	1	D	PSALM	68	23	D	PSALM	76	3	D
PSALM	53	2	D	PSALM	68	31	D	PSALM	76	5	D
PSALM	53	3	D	PSALM	68	32	D	PSALM	76	10	D
PSALM	53	4	D	PSALM	68	33	D	PSALM	76	11	D
PSALM	55	19	D	PSALM	68	34	D	PSALM	76	12	D
PSALM	55	20	D	PSALM	69	32	D	PSALM	78	1	D
PSALM	55	21	D	PSALM	69	33	D	PSALM	78	5	D
PSALM	55	21	D	PSALM	69	35	D	PSALM	78	6	D
PSALM	55	21	D	PSALM	69	36	D	PSALM	78	7	D
PSALM	55	22	D	PSALM	72	2	D	PSALM	78	8	D
PSALM	55	23	D	PSALM	72	3	D	PSALM	78	9	D
PSALM	55	23	D	PSALM	72	4	D	PSALM	78	10	D
PSALM	57	3	D	PSALM	72	5	D	PSALM	78	11	D
PSALM	58	3	D	PSALM	72	6	D	PSALM	78	12	D
PSALM	58	4	D	PSALM	72	7	D	PSALM	78	13	D
PSALM	58	5	D	PSALM	72	8	D	PSALM	78	14	D
PSALM	58	9	D	PSALM	72	9	D	PSALM	78	15	D
PSALM	58	10	D	PSALM	72	10	D	PSALM	78	16	D
PSALM	58	12	D	PSALM	72	11	D	PSALM	78	17	D
PSALM	62	6	D	PSALM	72	12	D	PSALM	78	18	D
PSALM	62	7	D	PSALM	72	13	D	PSALM	78	19	D
PSALM	62	8	D	PSALM	72	14	D	PSALM	78	20	D
PSALM	62	9	D	PSALM	72	15	D	PSALM	78	21	D
PSALM	62	10	D	PSALM	72	16	D	PSALM	78	22	D
PSALM	62	11	D	PSALM	72	20	D	PSALM	78	23	D
PSALM	64	7	D	PSALM	73	1	D	PSALM	78	24	D
PSALM	64	8	D	PSALM	73	2	D	PSALM	78	25	D
PSALM	64	9	D	PSALM	73	3	D	PSALM	78	26	D
PSALM	64	10	D	PSALM	73	4	D	PSALM	78	27	D
PSALM	65	6	D	PSALM	73	5	D	PSALM	78	28	D
PSALM	66	1	D	PSALM	73	6	D	PSALM	78	29	D
PSALM	66	2	D	PSALM	73	7	D	PSALM	78	30	D
PSALM	66	3	D	PSALM	73	8	D	PSALM	78	31	D
PSALM	66	4	D	PSALM	73	9	D	PSALM	78	32	D
PSALM	66	5	D	PSALM	73	10	D	PSALM	78	33	D
PSALM	66	6	D	PSALM	73	11	D	PSALM	78	34	D
PSALM	66	7	D	PSALM	73	12	D	PSALM	78	35	D
PSALM	66	18	D	PSALM	73	13	D	PSALM	78	36	D
PSALM	68	3	D	PSALM	73	14	D	PSALM	78	37	D
PSALM	68	4	D	PSALM	73	15	D	PSALM	78	38	D
PSALM	68	5	D	PSALM	73	16	D	PSALM	78	39	D
PSALM	68	6	D	PSALM	73	17	D	PSALM	78	40	D
PSALM	68	13	D	PSALM	73	28	D	PSALM	78	41	D
PSALM	68	15	D	PSALM	75	3	D	PSALM	78	42	D
PSALM	68	16	D	PSALM	75	5	D	PSALM	78	43	D
PSALM	68	17	D	PSALM	75	6	D	PSALM	78	44	D

PSALM	78	45	D	PSALM	91	1	D	PSALM	97	6	D
PSALM	78	46	D	PSALM	91	3	D	PSALM	97	7	D
PSALM	78	47	D	PSALM	91	4	D	PSALM	97	8	D
PSALM	78	48	D	PSALM	91	5	D	PSALM	97	9	D
PSALM	78	49	D	PSALM	91	6	D	PSALM	97	10	D
PSALM	78	50	D	PSALM	91	7	D	PSALM	97	11	D
PSALM	78	51	D	PSALM	91	8	D	PSALM	97	12	D
PSALM	78	52	D	PSALM	91	9	D	PSALM	98	1	D
PSALM	78	53	D	PSALM	91	10	D	PSALM	98	2	D
PSALM	78	54	D	PSALM	91	11	D	PSALM	98	3	D
PSALM	78	55	D	PSALM	91	12	D	PSALM	98	4	D
PSALM	78	56	D	PSALM	91	13	D	PSALM	98	5	D
PSALM	78	57	D	PSALM	92	1	D	PSALM	98	6	D
PSALM	78	58	D	PSALM	92	12	D	PSALM	98	7	D
PSALM	78	59	D	PSALM	92	13	D	PSALM	98	8	D
PSALM	78	60	D	PSALM	92	14	D	PSALM	98	9	D
PSALM	78	61	D	PSALM	92	15	D	PSALM	99	1	D
PSALM	78	62	D	PSALM	93	1	D	PSALM	99	2	D
PSALM	78	63	D	PSALM	94	11	D	PSALM	99	3	D
PSALM	78	64	D	PSALM	94	14	D	PSALM	99	4	D
PSALM	78	65	D	PSALM	94	15	D	PSALM	99	5	D
PSALM	78	66	D	PSALM	94	17	D	PSALM	99	6	D
PSALM	78	67	D	PSALM	95	3	D	PSALM	99	7	D
PSALM	78	68	D	PSALM	95	4	D	PSALM	99	8	D
PSALM	78	69	D	PSALM	95	5	D	PSALM	99	9	D
PSALM	78	70	D	PSALM	95	6	D	PSALM	100	1	D
PSALM	78	71	D	PSALM	95	7	D	PSALM	100	2	D
PSALM	78	72	D	PSALM	95	8	D	PSALM	100	3	D
PSALM	81	15	D	PSALM	95	9	D	PSALM	100	4	D
PSALM	81	16	D	PSALM	95	10	D	PSALM	100	5	D
PSALM	82	1	D	PSALM	95	11	D	PSALM	102	25	D
PSALM	82	3	D	PSALM	96	1	D	PSALM	103	6	D
PSALM	82	4	D	PSALM	96	2	D	PSALM	103	8	D
PSALM	84	7	D	PSALM	96	3	D	PSALM	103	9	D
PSALM	85	7	D	PSALM	96	4	D	PSALM	103	10	D
PSALM	85	8	D	PSALM	96	5	D	PSALM	103	11	D
PSALM	85	9	D	PSALM	96	6	D	PSALM	103	12	D
PSALM	85	10	D	PSALM	96	7	D	PSALM	103	13	D
PSALM	85	11	D	PSALM	96	8	D	PSALM	103	14	D
PSALM	85	12	D	PSALM	96	9	D	PSALM	103	15	D
PSALM	85	13	D	PSALM	96	10	D	PSALM	103	16	D
PSALM	87	1	D	PSALM	96	11	D	PSALM	103	17	D
PSALM	87	2	D	PSALM	96	12	D	PSALM	103	18	D
PSALM	87	5	D	PSALM	96	13	D	PSALM	103	19	D
PSALM	87	6	D	PSALM	97	1	D	PSALM	104	1	D
PSALM	87	7	D	PSALM	97	2	D	PSALM	104	2	D
PSALM	90	3	D	PSALM	97	3	D	PSALM	104	3	D
PSALM	90	4	D	PSALM	97	4	D	PSALM	104	4	D
PSALM	90	10	D	PSALM	97	5	D	PSALM	104	5	D

PSALM	104	6	D	PSALM	108	8	D	PSALM	127	4	D
PSALM	104	7	D	PSALM	108	9	D	PSALM	127	5	D
PSALM	104	8	D	PSALM	108	13	D	PSALM	128	1	D
PSALM	104	9	D	PSALM	110	2	D	PSALM	128	2	D
PSALM	104	10	D	PSALM	110	3	D	PSALM	128	3	D
PSALM	104	11	D	PSALM	110	4	D	PSALM	128	4	D
PSALM	104	12	D	PSALM	110	5	D	PSALM	128	5	D
PSALM	104	13	D	PSALM	110	6	D	PSALM	128	6	D
PSALM	104	14	D	PSALM	110	7	D	PSALM	132	11	D
PSALM	104	15	D	PSALM	111	8	D	PSALM	132	12	D
PSALM	104	16	D	PSALM	111	10	D	PSALM	132	13	D
PSALM	104	17	D	PSALM	112	2	D	PSALM	132	14	D
PSALM	104	18	D	PSALM	112	3	D	PSALM	132	15	D
PSALM	104	19	D	PSALM	112	4	D	PSALM	132	16	D
PSALM	104	20	D	PSALM	112	5	D	PSALM	132	17	D
PSALM	104	21	D	PSALM	112	6	D	PSALM	132	18	D
PSALM	104	22	D	PSALM	112	7	D				
PSALM	104	23	D	PSALM	112	8	D				
PSALM	104	24	D	PSALM	112	9	D				
PSALM	104	25	D	PSALM	112	10	D				
PSALM	104	26	D	PSALM	113	4	D				
PSALM	104	27	D	PSALM	114	7	D				
PSALM	104	28	D	PSALM	114	8	D				
PSALM	104	29	D	PSALM	115	3	D				
PSALM	104	30	D	PSALM	115	4	D				
PSALM	104	31	D	PSALM	115	5	D				
PSALM	104	32	D	PSALM	115	6	D				
PSALM	104	33	D	PSALM	115	7	D				
PSALM	104	34	D	PSALM	115	8	D				
PSALM	104	35	D	PSALM	115	9	D				
PSALM	105	4	D	PSALM	115	10	D				
PSALM	105	7	D	PSALM	115	11	D				
PSALM	107	2	D	PSALM	115	12	D				
PSALM	107	3	D	PSALM	115	13	D				
PSALM	107	9	D	PSALM	115	14	D				
PSALM	107	22	D	PSALM	115	15	D				
PSALM	107	32	D	PSALM	115	16	D				
PSALM	107	33	D	PSALM	116	15	D				
PSALM	107	34	D	PSALM	118	7	D				
PSALM	107	35	D	PSALM	118	8	D				
PSALM	107	36	D	PSALM	118	9	D				
PSALM	107	37	D	PSALM	118	14	D				
PSALM	107	38	D	PSALM	118	15	D				
PSALM	107	39	D	PSALM	118	16	D				
PSALM	107	40	D	PSALM	118	17	D				
PSALM	107	41	D	PSALM	119	4	D				
PSALM	107	42	D	PSALM	127	1	D				
PSALM	107	43	D	PSALM	127	2	D				
PSALM	108	7	D	PSALM	127	3	D				

PSALM	3	1	G	PSALM	41	12	G	PSALM	64	6	G
PSALM	5	9	G	PSALM	42	3	G	PSALM	65	3	G
PSALM	6	3	G	PSALM	42	5	G	PSALM	69	2	G
PSALM	6	4	G	PSALM	42	6	G	PSALM	69	3	G
PSALM	6	5	G	PSALM	41	11	G	PSALM	69	4	G
PSALM	6	6	G	PSALM	42	7	G	PSALM	69	7	G
PSALM	6	7	G	PSALM	42	9	G	PSALM	69	8	G
PSALM	6	8	G	PSALM	42	10	G	PSALM	69	10	G
PSALM	6	9	G	PSALM	42	11	G	PSALM	69	11	G
PSALM	6	10	G	PSALM	43	2	G	PSALM	69	12	G
PSALM	7	1	G	PSALM	43	5	G	PSALM	69	19	G
PSALM	7	2	G	PSALM	44	9	G	PSALM	69	20	G
PSALM	7	3	G	PSALM	44	10	G	PSALM	69	26	G
PSALM	10	1	G	PSALM	44	11	G	PSALM	73	1	G
PSALM	10	5	G	PSALM	44	12	G	PSALM	73	2	G
PSALM	11	3	G	PSALM	44	13	G	PSALM	73	3	G
PSALM	13	1	G	PSALM	44	14	G	PSALM	73	4	G
PSALM	13	2	G	PSALM	44	15	G	PSALM	73	5	G
PSALM	22	6	G	PSALM	44	16	G	PSALM	73	6	G
PSALM	22	7	G	PSALM	44	24	G	PSALM	73	7	G
PSALM	22	12	G	PSALM	44	25	G	PSALM	73	8	G
PSALM	31	11	G	PSALM	50	14	G	PSALM	73	9	G
PSALM	31	12	G	PSALM	50	23	G	PSALM	73	10	G
PSALM	31	13	G	PSALM	54	2	G	PSALM	73	11	G
PSALM	32	3	G	PSALM	55	1	G	PSALM	73	12	G
PSALM	32	4	G	PSALM	55	2	G	PSALM	73	13	G
PSALM	35	12	G	PSALM	55	3	G	PSALM	73	14	G
PSALM	35	13	G	PSALM	55	4	G	PSALM	73	15	G
PSALM	35	14	G	PSALM	55	5	G	PSALM	73	16	G
PSALM	35	15	G	PSALM	55	6	G	PSALM	73	21	G
PSALM	35	16	G	PSALM	55	7	G	PSALM	73	22	G
PSALM	35	20	G	PSALM	55	8	G	PSALM	73	23	G
PSALM	35	21	G	PSALM	55	10	G	PSALM	73	24	G
PSALM	38	1	G	PSALM	55	11	G	PSALM	73	25	G
PSALM	38	2	G	PSALM	55	12	G	PSALM	73	26	G
PSALM	38	3	G	PSALM	55	13	G	PSALM	73	27	G
PSALM	38	4	G	PSALM	55	14	G	PSALM	74	1	G
PSALM	38	5	G	PSALM	56	5	G	PSALM	74	4	G
PSALM	38	6	G	PSALM	56	6	G	PSALM	74	5	G
PSALM	38	7	G	PSALM	56	8	G	PSALM	74	6	G
PSALM	38	8	G	PSALM	57	4	G	PSALM	74	7	G
PSALM	40	12	G	PSALM	57	6	G	PSALM	74	8	G
PSALM	40	17	G	PSALM	60	1	G	PSALM	74	9	G
PSALM	41	5	G	PSALM	60	2	G	PSALM	74	10	G
PSALM	41	6	G	PSALM	60	3	G	PSALM	74	11	G
PSALM	41	7	G	PSALM	64	2	G	PSALM	77	4	G
PSALM	41	8	G	PSALM	64	3	G	PSALM	77	7	G
PSALM	41	9	G	PSALM	64	4	G	PSALM	77	8	G
PSALM	41	10	G	PSALM	64	5	G	PSALM	77	9	G

PSALM	79	1	G	PSALM	94	7	G	PSALM	143	3	G
PSALM	79	2	G	PSALM	94	16	G	PSALM	143	4	G
PSALM	79	3	G	PSALM	101	2	G	PSALM	143	5	G
PSALM	79	4	G	PSALM	102	3	G	PSALM	143	6	G
PSALM	79	5	G	PSALM	102	4	G	PSALM	143	7	G
PSALM	79	6	G	PSALM	102	5	G	PSALM	143	8	G
PSALM	79	7	G	PSALM	102	6	G	PSALM	143	9	G
PSALM	79	8	G	PSALM	102	7	G	PSALM	143	10	G
PSALM	79	9	G	PSALM	102	8	G	PSALM	143	11	G
PSALM	79	10	G	PSALM	102	9	G	PSALM	143	12	G
PSALM	79	11	G	PSALM	102	10	G				
PSALM	79	12	G	PSALM	102	11	G	Hanna's	Prayer		
PSALM	80	4	G	PSALM	102	23	G	PSALM	113	7 & 8	
PSALM	80	5	G	PSALM	102	24	G				
PSALM	80	12	G	PSALM	107	8	G				
PSALM	80	13	G	PSALM	107	15	G				
PSALM	80	16	G	PSALM	107	21	G				
PSALM	85	4	G	PSALM	107	31	G				
PSALM	85	5	G	PSALM	118	18	G				
PSALM	86	14	G	PSALM	119	5	G				
PSALM	88	1	G	PSALM	119	6	G				
PSALM	88	3	G	PSALM	119	7	G				
PSALM	88	4	G	PSALM	119	8	G				
PSALM	88	5	G	PSALM	119	25	G				
PSALM	88	6	G	PSALM	119	28	G				
PSALM	88	7	G	PSALM	120	1	G				
PSALM	88	8	G	PSALM	123	4	G				
PSALM	88	9	G	PSALM	129	1	G				
PSALM	88	13	G	PSALM	129	2	G				
PSALM	88	14	G	PSALM	129	3	G				
PSALM	88	15	G	PSALM	129	4	G				
PSALM	88	16	G	PSALM	130	1	G				
PSALM	88	17	G	PSALM	130	2	G				
PSALM	88	18	G	PSALM	139	20	G				
PSALM	89	37	G	PSALM	139	21	G				
PSALM	89	38	G	PSALM	139	22	G				
PSALM	89	39	G	PSALM	141	6	G				
PSALM	89	40	G	PSALM	141	7	G				
PSALM	89	41	G	PSALM	141	8	G				
PSALM	89	42	G	PSALM	141	9	G				
PSALM	89	43	G	PSALM	141	10	G				
PSALM	89	44	G	PSALM	142	1	G				
PSALM	89	45	G	PSALM	142	2	G				
PSALM	90	7	G	PSALM	142	3	G				
PSALM	90	8	G	PSALM	142	4	G				
PSALM	90	9	G	PSALM	142	5	G				
PSALM	94	5	G	PSALM	142	6	G				
PSALM	94	6	G	PSALM	142	7	G				

PSALM	2	6	M	PSALM	39	2	M
PSALM	2	7	M	PSALM	39	9	M
PSALM	2	8	M	PSALM	40	6	M
PSALM	16	10	M	PSALM	40	7	M
PSALM	16	11	M	PSALM	41	5	M
PSALM	21	2	M	PSALM	41	6	M
PSALM	21	3	M	PSALM	41	7	M
PSALM	21	4	M	PSALM	41	8	M
PSALM	21	5	M	PSALM	41	9	M
PSALM	21	6	M	PSALM	41	10	M
PSALM	21	12	M	PSALM	41	11	M
PSALM	21	11	M	PSALM	41	12	M
PSALM	21	13	M	PSALM	45	6	M
PSALM	22	1	M	PSALM	45	7	M
PSALM	22	2	M	PSALM	49	3	M
PSALM	22	3	M	PSALM	55	12	M
PSALM	22	6	M	PSALM	55	13	M
PSALM	22	7	M	PSALM	55	14	M
PSALM	22	8	M	PSALM	69	9	M
PSALM	22	9	M	PSALM	69	21	M
PSALM	22	12	M	PSALM	72	17	M
PSALM	22	13	M	PSALM	89	3	M
PSALM	22	14	M	PSALM	89	4	M
PSALM	22	15	M	PSALM	89	24	M
PSALM	22	16	M	PSALM	102	25	M
PSALM	22	17	M	PSALM	102	26	M
PSALM	22	18	M	PSALM	102	27	M
PSALM	22	22	M	PSALM	109	6	M
PSALM	31	5	M	PSALM	109	7	M
PSALM	34	20	M	PSALM	109	8	M
PSALM	35	11	M	PSALM	109	25	M
PSALM	38	8	M	PSALM	109	26	M
PSALM	38	9	M	PSALM	109	27	M
PSALM	38	10	M	PSALM	110	1	M
PSALM	38	11	M	PSALM	118	22	M
PSALM	38	12	M	PSALM	118	23	M
PSALM	38	13	M	PSALM	118	24	M
PSALM	38	14	M	PSALM	132	11	M
PSALM	38	15	M	PSALM	132	12	M
PSALM	38	16	M	PSALM	132	13	M
PSALM	38	17	M	PSALM	132	14	M
PSALM	38	18	M	PSALM	132	15	M
PSALM	38	19	M	PSALM	132	16	M
PSALM	38	20	M	PSALM	132	17	M
PSALM	38	21	M	PSALM	132	18	M
PSALM	38	22	M				

Prayer to Hear My Prayer and Teach

PSALM	4	1	P.7	PSALM	74	2	P.7
PSALM	5	1	P.7	PSALM	74	3	P.7
PSALM	5	2	P.7	PSALM	74	20	P.7
PSALM	5	8	P.7	PSALM	84	8	P.7
PSALM	13	3	P.7	PSALM	86	1	P.7
PSALM	17	1	P.7	PSALM	86	2	P.7
PSALM	17	2	P.7	PSALM	86	3	P.7
PSALM	17	6	P.7	PSALM	86	6	P.7
PSALM	19	14	P.7	PSALM	86	11	P.7
PSALM	20	1	P.7	PSALM	88	2	P.7
PSALM	20	5	P.7	PSALM	102	1	P.7
PSALM	20	6	P.7	PSALM	102	2	P.7
PSALM	25	4	P.7	PSALM	119	12	P.7
PSALM	25	5	P.7	PSALM	119	18	P.7
PSALM	27	7	P.7	PSALM	119	19	P.7
PSALM	27	9	P.7	PSALM	119	26	P.7
PSALM	27	11	P.7	PSALM	119	27	P.7
PSALM	28	1	P.7	PSALM	119	33	P.7
PSALM	28	2	P.7	PSALM	119	34	P.7
PSALM	30	10	P.7	PSALM	119	66	P.7
PSALM	31	1	P.7	PSALM	119	68	P.7
PSALM	31	2	P.7	PSALM	119	73	P.7
PSALM	43	3	P.7	PSALM	119	108	P.7
PSALM	48	11	P.7	PSALM	119	124	P.7
PSALM	54	1	P.7	PSALM	119	125	P.7
PSALM	61	1	P.7	PSALM	119	135	P.7
PSALM	61	2	P.7	PSALM	119	144	P.7
PSALM	61	3	P.7	PSALM	140	6	P.7
PSALM	61	4	P.7	PSALM	141	1	P.7
PSALM	61	5	P.7	PSALM	141	2	P.7
PSALM	64	1	P.7	PSALM	144	11	P.7
PSALM	69	6	P.7	PSALM	144	12	P.7
PSALM	71	1	P.7	PSALM	144	13	P.7
				PSALM	144	14	P.7

PSALM	7	4	P.3
PSALM	7	5	P.3
PSALM	16	1	P.3
PSALM	19	12	P.3
PSALM	19	13	P.3
PSALM	25	7	P.3
PSALM	25	11	P.3
PSALM	25	16	P.3
PSALM	25	18	P.3
PSALM	25	20	P.3
PSALM	31	9	P.3
PSALM	39	4	P.3
PSALM	39	5	P.3
PSALM	39	7	P.3
PSALM	39	8	P.3
PSALM	39	10	P.3
PSALM	40	11	P.3
PSALM	40	13	P.3
PSALM	51	1	P.3
PSALM	51	2	P.3
PSALM	51	7	P.3
PSALM	51	9	P.3
PSALM	51	10	P.3
PSALM	71	9	P.3
PSALM	79	8	P.3
PSALM	79	9	P.3
PSALM	90	12	P.3
PSALM	90	13	P.3
PSALM	90	14	P.3
PSALM	119	9	P.3
PSALM	119	29	P.3
PSALM	119	36	P.3
PSALM	119	37	P.3
PSALM	119	43	P.3
PSALM	119	77	P.3
PSALM	119	133	P.3
PSALM	119	176	P.3
PSALM	130	3	P.3
PSALM	141	3	P.3
PSALM	141	4	P.3
PSALM	141	5	P.3

Prayer for Peace and Calm

PSALM	6	1	P.2	PSALM	89	48	P.2
PSALM	12	1	P.2	PSALM	89	49	P.2
PSALM	12	2	P.2	PSALM	89	50	P.2
PSALM	12	7	P.2	PSALM	89	51	P.2
PSALM	17	8	P.2	PSALM	108	6	P.2
PSALM	17	9	P.2	PSALM	108	12	P.2
PSALM	20	9	P.2	PSALM	119	10	P.2
PSALM	22	11	P.2	PSALM	119	11	P.2
PSALM	22	19	P.2	PSALM	119	21	P.2
PSALM	25	22	P.2	PSALM	119	22	P.2
PSALM	26	2	P.2	PSALM	119	31	P 2
PSALM	26	11	P.2	PSALM	119	42	P 2
PSALM	31	3	P.2	PSALM	119	49	P 2
PSALM	31	16	P.2	PSALM	119	76	P 2
PSALM	33	22	P.2	PSALM	119	80	P.2
PSALM	40	17	P.2	PSALM	119	81	P.2
PSALM	51	8	P.2	PSALM	119	116	P.2
PSALM	51	11	P.2	PSALM	119	117	P.2
PSALM	51	12	P.2	PSALM	119	132	P.2
PSALM	51	16	P.2	PSALM	119	153	P.2
PSALM	51	17	P.2	PSALM	119	169	P.2
PSALM	51	18	P.2	PSALM	119	170	P.2
PSALM	56	3	P.2	PSALM	119	173	P.2
PSALM	57	1	P.2	PSALM	123	1	P.2
PSALM	68	3	P.2	PSALM	123	2	P.2
PSALM	69	1	P.2	PSALM	123	3	P.2
PSALM	79	11	P.2	PSALM	126	4	P.2
PSALM	86	4	P.2	PSALM	130	4	P.2
PSALM	86	17	P.2	PSALM	131	1	P 2
PSALM	89	47	P.2	PSALM	131	2	P 2

Prayer for Prosperity and Stability

PSALM	4	3	P.1	PSALM	106	47	P.1
PSALM	4	4	P.1	PSALM	109	21	P.1
PSALM	4	5	P.1	PSALM	109	22	P.1
PSALM	16	3	P.1	PSALM	109	23	P.1
PSALM	17	5	P.1	PSALM	109	24	P.1
PSALM	17	7	P.1	PSALM	109	28	P.1
PSALM	25	6	P.1	PSALM	118	25	P.1
PSALM	25	21	P.1	PSALM	119	17	P.1
PSALM	26	1	P.1	PSALM	119	38	P.1
PSALM	28	9	P.1	PSALM	119	40	P.1
PSALM	31	4	P.1	PSALM	119	41	P.1
PSALM	36	10	P.1	PSALM	119	88	P.1
PSALM	36	11	P.1	PSALM	119	107	P.1
PSALM	60	11	P.1	PSALM	119	149	P.1
PSALM	68	28	P.1	PSALM	119	156	P.1
PSALM	69	29	P.1	PSALM	119	159	P.1
PSALM	72	1	P.1	PSALM	119	174	P.1
PSALM	85	6	P.1	PSALM	119	175	P.1
PSALM	85	7	P.1	PSALM	122	6	P.1
PSALM	86	16	P.1	PSALM	122	7	P.1
PSALM	90	15	P.1	PSALM	122	8	P.1
PSALM	90	16	P.1	PSALM	125	4	P.1
PSALM	90	17	P.1	PSALM	125	5	P.1
PSALM	106	4	P.1	PSALM	132	1	P.1
PSALM	106	5	P.1	PSALM	132	2	P.1
				PSALM	138	8	P.1

Prayer for Spreading the Gospel

PSALM	2	8	P.4
PSALM	8	1	P.4
PSALM	9	1	P.4
PSALM	9	14	P.4
PSALM	25	17	P.4
PSALM	40	16	P.4
PSALM	51	13	P.4
PSALM	51	14	P.4
PSALM	51	15	P.4
PSALM	57	11	P.4
PSALM	67	1	P.4
PSALM	67	2	P.4
PSALM	67	3	P.4
PSALM	67	4	P.4
PSALM	67	5	P.4
PSALM	67	6	P.4
PSALM	67	7	P.4
PSALM	71	8	P.4
PSALM	71	18	P.4
PSALM	79	10	P.4
PSALM	88	10	P.4
PSALM	88	11	P.4
PSALM	89	46	P.4
PSALM	108	5	P.4
PSALM	115	1	P.4
PSALM	115	2	P.4
PSALM	119	35	P.4
PSALM	119	46	P.4
PSALM	119	79	P.4
PSALM	132	8	P.4
PSALM	132	9	P.4
PSALM	132	10	P.4

PSALM	5	10	P.5	PSALM	83	11	P.5
PSALM	5	11	P.5	PSALM	83	12	P.5
PSALM	9	20	P.5	PSALM	83	13	P.5
PSALM	10	15	P.5	PSALM	83	14	P.5
PSALM	21	13	P.5	PSALM	83	15	P.5
PSALM	55	15	P.5	PSALM	83	16	P.5
PSALM	56	7	P.5	PSALM	83	17	P.5
PSALM	57	5	P.5	PSALM	83	18	P.5
PSALM	58	6	P.5	PSALM	94	1	P.5
PSALM	58	7	P.5	PSALM	94	2	P.5
PSALM	58	8	P.5	PSALM	94	3	P.5
PSALM	68	1	P.5	PSALM	94	4	P.5
PSALM	68	2	P.5	PSALM	109	9	P.5
PSALM	68	30	P.5	PSALM	109	11	P.5
PSALM	79	12	P.5	PSALM	109	12	P.5
PSALM	80	1	P.5	PSALM	109	13	P.5
PSALM	80	2	P.5	PSALM	109	14	P.5
PSALM	80	3	P.5	PSALM	109	15	P.5
PSALM	80	6	P.5	PSALM	109	16	P.5
PSALM	80	7	P.5	PSALM	109	17	P.5
PSALM	80	14	P.5	PSALM	109	18	P.5
PSALM	80	15	P.5	PSALM	109	19	P.5
PSALM	80	17	P.5	PSALM	109	20	P.5
PSALM	80	19	P.5	PSALM	109	29	P.5
PSALM	82	8	P.5	PSALM	137	7	P.5
PSALM	83	1	P.5	PSALM	137	8	P.5
PSALM	83	2	P.5	PSALM	137	9	P.5
PSALM	83	3	P.5	PSALM	140	10	P.5
PSALM	83	4	P.5	PSALM	140	11	P.5
PSALM	83	5	P.5	PSALM	140	12	P.5
PSALM	83	6	P.5	PSALM	140	12	P.5
PSALM	83	7	P.5	PSALM	140	13	P.5
PSALM	83	8	P.5	PSALM	144	3	P.5
PSALM	83	9	P.5	PSALM	144	4	P.5
PSALM	83	10	P.5	PSALM	144	5	P.5

Prayer to be Saved from Enemies

PSALM	56	2	P.6	PSALM	71	13	P.6
PSALM	59	1	P.6	PSALM	74	18	P.6
PSALM	59	2	P.6	PSALM	74	19	P.6
PSALM	59	3	P.6	PSALM	74	21	P.6
PSALM	59	4	P.6	PSALM	74	22	P.6
PSALM	59	5	P.6	PSALM	74	23	P.6
PSALM	59	6	P.6	PSALM	109	1	P.6
PSALM	59	7	P.6	PSALM	109	2	P.6
PSALM	59	11	P.6	PSALM	109	3	P.6
PSALM	59	12	P.6	PSALM	109	4	P.6
PSALM	59	13	P.6	PSALM	109	5	P.6
PSALM	59	14	P.6	PSALM	119	39	P.6
PSALM	59	15	P.6	PSALM	119	78	P.6
PSALM	60	5	P.6	PSALM	119	84	P.6
PSALM	69	14	P.6	PSALM	119	85	P.6
PSALM	69	15	P.6	PSALM	119	86	P.6
PSALM	69	16	P.6	PSALM	119	87	P.6
PSALM	69	17	P.6	PSALM	119	94	P.6
PSALM	69	18	P.6	PSALM	119	121	P.6
PSALM	69	22	P.6	PSALM	119	122	P.6
PSALM	69	23	P.6	PSALM	119	134	P.6
PSALM	69	24	P.6	PSALM	119	154	P.6
PSALM	69	25	P.6	PSALM	120	2	P.6
PSALM	69	27	P.6	PSALM	129	5	P.6
PSALM	69	28	P.6	PSALM	129	6	P.6
PSALM	70	1	P.6	PSALM	129	7	P.6
PSALM	70	2	P.6	PSALM	129	8	P.6
PSALM	70	3	P.6	PSALM	140	1	P.6
PSALM	70	4	P.6	PSALM	140	2	P.6
PSALM	70	5	P.6	PSALM	140	3	P.6
PSALM	71	2	P.6	PSALM	140	4	P.6
PSALM	71	3	P.6	PSALM	140	5	P.6
PSALM	71	4	P.6	PSALM	140	8	P.6
PSALM	71	10	P.6	PSALM	140	9	P.6
PSALM	71	11	P.6	PSALM	144	6	P.6
PSALM	71	12	P.6	PSALM	144	7	P.6
				PSALM	144	8	P.6

Rebuke

PSALM	2	1	R
PSALM	2	2	R
PSALM	2	3	R
PSALM	2	10	R
PSALM	2	11	R
PSALM	4	2	R
PSALM	4	3	R
PSALM	4	6	R
PSALM	52	1	R
PSALM	52	2	R
PSALM	52	3	R
PSALM	52	4	R
PSALM	52	5	R
PSALM	58	1	R
PSALM	58	2	R
PSALM	62	3	R
PSALM	62	4	R
PSALM	82	2	R
PSALM	94	8	R
PSALM	94	9	R
PSALM	94	10	R
PSALM	107	10	R
PSALM	107	11	R
PSALM	107	12	R
PSALM	120	3	R
PSALM	120	4	R
PSALM	120	5	R
PSALM	120	6	R
PSALM	120	7	R

PSALM	8	8	S
PSALM	19	1	S
PSALM	19	2	S
PSALM	19	3	S
PSALM	24	2	S
PSALM	36	9	S
PSALM	78	25	S
PSALM	82	5	S
PSALM	135	7	S
PSALM	136	5	S
PSALM	136	6	S
PSALM	136	7	S
PSALM	136	8	S
PSALM	136	9	S
PSALM	136	13	S
PSALM	136	14	S
PSALM	136	15	S
PSALM	136	16	S
PSALM	136	25	S
PSALM	147	4	S
PSALM	147	8	S
PSALM	147	16	S
PSALM	147	17	S
PSALM	147	18	S

PSALM	3	4	TSR	PSALM	22	5	TSR	PSALM	40	3	TSR
PSALM	3	5	TSR	PSALM	22	24	TSR	PSALM	40	4	TSR
PSALM	3	6	TSR	PSALM	22	25	TSR	PSALM	40	8	TSR
PSALM	3	7	TSR	PSALM	23	1	TSR	PSALM	40	9	TSR
PSALM	9	6	TSR	PSALM	23	2	TSR	PSALM	40	10	TSR
PSALM	11	1	TSR	PSALM	23	3	TSR	PSALM	40	17	TSR
PSALM	14	5	TSR	PSALM	26	3	TSR	PSALM	42	4	TSR
PSALM	14	6	TSR	PSALM	26	4	TSR	PSALM	43	4	TSR
PSALM	14	7	TSR	PSALM	26	5	TSR	PSALM	44	1	TSR
PSALM	16	4	TSR	PSALM	26	6	TSR	PSALM	44	2	TSR
PSALM	16	6	TSR	PSALM	26	7	TSR	PSALM	44	3	TSR
PSALM	16	7	TSR	PSALM	26	8	TSR	PSALM	44	5	TSR
PSALM	16	8	TSR	PSALM	26	12	TSR	PSALM	44	6	TSR
PSALM	16	9	TSR	PSALM	27	1	TSR	PSALM	44	7	TSR
PSALM	17	10	TSR	PSALM	27	2	TSR	PSALM	44	8	TSR
PSALM	17	11	TSR	PSALM	27	3	TSR	PSALM	44	17	TSR
PSALM	17	12	TSR	PSALM	27	4	TSR	PSALM	44	18	TSR
PSALM	18	1	TSR	PSALM	27	5	TSR	PSALM	44	19	TSR
PSALM	18	2	TSR	PSALM	27	6	TSR	PSALM	44	20	TSR
PSALM	18	3	TSR	PSALM	27	8	TSR	PSALM	45	1	TSR
PSALM	18	4	TSR	PSALM	27	10	TSR	PSALM	48	9	TSR
PSALM	18	5	TSR	PSALM	27	13	TSR	PSALM	48	10	TSR
PSALM	18	6	TSR	PSALM	30	2	TSR	PSALM	49	3	TSR
PSALM	18	16	TSR	PSALM	30	3	TSR	PSALM	53	5	TSR
PSALM	18	17	TSR	PSALM	30	4	TSR	PSALM	53	6	TSR
PSALM	18	18	TSR	PSALM	30	6	TSR	PSALM	54	6	TSR
PSALM	18	19	TSR	PSALM	30	7	TSR	PSALM	54	7	TSR
PSALM	18	20	TSR	PSALM	30	8	TSR	PSALM	55	16	TSR
PSALM	18	21	TSR	PSALM	30	9	TSR	PSALM	55	17	TSR
PSALM	18	22	TSR	PSALM	30	10	TSR	PSALM	55	18	TSR
PSALM	18	23	TSR	PSALM	30	11	TSR	PSALM	56	10	TSR
PSALM	18	24	TSR	PSALM	30	12	TSR	PSALM	56	11	TSR
PSALM	18	37	TSR	PSALM	31	6	TSR	PSALM	56	12	TSR
PSALM	18	38	TSR	PSALM	31	7	TSR	PSALM	56	13	TSR
PSALM	18	39	TSR	PSALM	31	8	TSR	PSALM	57	2	TSR
PSALM	18	42	TSR	PSALM	31	14	TSR	PSALM	57	7	TSR
PSALM	18	44	TSR	PSALM	31	20	TSR	PSALM	57	8	TSR
PSALM	18	45	TSR	PSALM	31	21	TSR	PSALM	57	9	TSR
PSALM	18	46	TSR	PSALM	31	22	TSR	PSALM	57	10	TSR
PSALM	18	47	TSR	PSALM	32	7	TSR	PSALM	59	16	TSR
PSALM	18	48	TSR	PSALM	33	20	TSR	PSALM	59	17	TSR
PSALM	18	50	TSR	PSALM	33	21	TSR	PSALM	66	17	TSR
PSALM	19	4	TSR	PSALM	34	4	TSR	PSALM	66	19	TSR
PSALM	19	5	TSR	PSALM	34	5	TSR	PSALM	68	8	TSR
PSALM	19	6	TSR	PSALM	34	6	TSR	PSALM	68	9	TSR
PSALM	20	7	TSR	PSALM	39	1	TSR	PSALM	68	10	TSR
PSALM	20	8	TSR	PSALM	39	3	TSR	PSALM	68	11	TSR
PSALM	21	7	TSR	PSALM	40	1	TSR	PSALM	68	12	TSR
PSALM	22	4	TSR	PSALM	40	2	TSR	PSALM	68	14	TSR

PSALM	68	25	TSR	PSALM	78	17	TSR	PSALM	78	66	TSR
PSALM	69	30	TSR	PSALM	78	18	TSR	PSALM	78	67	TSR
PSALM	69	31	TSR	PSALM	78	19	TSR	PSALM	78	68	TSR
PSALM	71	14	TSR	PSALM	78	20	TSR	PSALM	78	69	TSR
PSALM	71	15	TSR	PSALM	78	21	TSR	PSALM	78	70	TSR
PSALM	71	16	TSR	PSALM	78	22	TSR	PSALM	78	71	TSR
PSALM	71	23	TSR	PSALM	78	23	TSR	PSALM	78	72	TSR
PSALM	71	24	TSR	PSALM	78	24	TSR	PSALM	79	13	TSR
PSALM	74	12	TSR	PSALM	78	25	TSR	PSALM	80	8	TSR
PSALM	74	13	TSR	PSALM	78	26	TSR	PSALM	80	9	TSR
PSALM	74	14	TSR	PSALM	78	27	TSR	PSALM	80	10	TSR
PSALM	74	15	TSR	PSALM	78	28	TSR	PSALM	80	11	TSR
PSALM	74	16	TSR	PSALM	78	29	TSR	PSALM	80	18	TSR
PSALM	74	17	TSR	PSALM	78	30	TSR	PSALM	81	4	TSR
PSALM	75	2	TSR	PSALM	78	31	TSR	PSALM	81	5	TSR
PSALM	75	4	TSR	PSALM	78	32	TSR	PSALM	81	6	TSR
PSALM	75	8	TSR	PSALM	78	33	TSR	PSALM	81	7	TSR
PSALM	75	9	TSR	PSALM	78	34	TSR	PSALM	81	8	TSR
PSALM	75	10	TSR	PSALM	78	35	TSR	PSALM	81	9	TSR
PSALM	76	8	TSR	PSALM	78	36	TSR	PSALM	81	10	TSR
PSALM	76	9	TSR	PSALM	78	37	TSR	PSALM	81	11	TSR
PSALM	77	1	TSR	PSALM	78	38	TSR	PSALM	81	12	TSR
PSALM	77	2	TSR	PSALM	78	39	TSR	PSALM	81	13	TSR
PSALM	77	3	TSR	PSALM	78	40	TSR	PSALM	81	14	TSR
PSALM	77	5	TSR	PSALM	78	41	TSR	PSALM	82	6	TSR
PSALM	77	6	TSR	PSALM	78	42	TSR	PSALM	82	7	TSR
PSALM	77	10	TSR	PSALM	78	43	TSR	PSALM	85	1	TSR
PSALM	77	11	TSR	PSALM	78	44	TSR	PSALM	85	2	TSR
PSALM	77	12	TSR	PSALM	78	45	TSR	PSALM	85	3	TSR
PSALM	77	15	TSR	PSALM	78	46	TSR	PSALM	86	7	TSR
PSALM	77	16	TSR	PSALM	78	47	TSR	PSALM	87	4	TSR
PSALM	77	17	TSR	PSALM	78	48	TSR	PSALM	88	12	TSR
PSALM	77	18	TSR	PSALM	78	49	TSR	PSALM	89	25	TSR
PSALM	77	20	TSR	PSALM	78	50	TSR	PSALM	89	26	TSR
PSALM	78	2	TSR	PSALM	78	51	TSR	PSALM	89	27	TSR
PSALM	78	3	TSR	PSALM	78	52	TSR	PSALM	89	28	TSR
PSALM	78	4	TSR	PSALM	78	53	TSR	PSALM	89	29	TSR
PSALM	78	5	TSR	PSALM	78	54	TSR	PSALM	89	30	TSR
PSALM	78	6	TSR	PSALM	78	55	TSR	PSALM	89	31	TSR
PSALM	78	7	TSR	PSALM	78	56	TSR	PSALM	89	32	TSR
PSALM	78	8	TSR	PSALM	78	57	TSR	PSALM	89	33	TSR
PSALM	78	9	TSR	PSALM	78	58	TSR	PSALM	89	34	TSR
PSALM	78	10	TSR	PSALM	78	59	TSR	PSALM	89	35	TSR
PSALM	78	11	TSR	PSALM	78	60	TSR	PSALM	89	36	TSR
PSALM	78	12	TSR	PSALM	78	61	TSR	PSALM	91	2	TSR
PSALM	78	13	TSR	PSALM	78	62	TSR	PSALM	91	14	TSR
PSALM	78	14	TSR	PSALM	78	63	TSR	PSALM	91	15	TSR
PSALM	78	15	TSR	PSALM	78	64	TSR	PSALM	91	16	TSR
PSALM	78	16	TSR	PSALM	78	65	TSR	PSALM	92	15	TSR

PSALM	101	6	TSR	PSALM	105	41	TSR	PSALM	107	13	TSR
PSALM	101	7	TSR	PSALM	105	42	TSR	PSALM	107	14	TSR
PSALM	101	8	TSR	PSALM	105	43	TSR	PSALM	107	16	TSR
PSALM	102	13	TSR	PSALM	105	44	TSR	PSALM	107	17	TSR
PSALM	102	14	TSR	PSALM	105	45	TSR	PSALM	107	18	TSR
PSALM	102	15	TSR	PSALM	106	7	TSR	PSALM	107	19	TSR
PSALM	102	16	TSR	PSALM	106	8	TSR	PSALM	107	20	TSR
PSALM	102	17	TSR	PSALM	106	9	TSR	PSALM	107	23	TSR
PSALM	102	18	TSR	PSALM	106	10	TSR	PSALM	107	24	TSR
PSALM	102	19	TSR	PSALM	106	11	TSR	PSALM	107	25	TSR
PSALM	102	20	TSR	PSALM	106	12	TSR	PSALM	107	26	TSR
PSALM	102	21	TSR	PSALM	106	13	TSR	PSALM	107	27	TSR
PSALM	102	22	TSR	PSALM	106	14	TSR	PSALM	107	28	TSR
PSALM	103	7	TSR	PSALM	106	15	TSR	PSALM	107	29	TSR
PSALM	105	5	TSR	PSALM	106	16	TSR	PSALM	107	30	TSR
PSALM	105	6	TSR	PSALM	106	17	TSR	PSALM	111	4	TSR
PSALM	105	8	TSR	PSALM	106	18	TSR	PSALM	111	5	TSR
PSALM	105	9	TSR	PSALM	106	19	TSR	PSALM	111	6	TSR
PSALM	105	10	TSR	PSALM	106	20	TSR	PSALM	111	9	TSR
PSALM	105	11	TSR	PSALM	106	21	TSR	PSALM	114	1	TSR
PSALM	105	12	TSR	PSALM	106	22	TSR	PSALM	114	2	TSR
PSALM	105	13	TSR	PSALM	106	23	TSR	PSALM	114	3	TSR
PSALM	105	14	TSR	PSALM	106	24	TSR	PSALM	114	4	TSR
PSALM	105	15	TSR	PSALM	106	25	TSR	PSALM	114	5	TSR
PSALM	105	16	TSR	PSALM	106	26	TSR	PSALM	114	6	TSR
PSALM	105	17	TSR	PSALM	106	27	TSR	PSALM	116	1	TSR
PSALM	105	18	TSR	PSALM	106	28	TSR	PSALM	116	2	TSR
PSALM	105	19	TSR	PSALM	106	29	TSR	PSALM	116	3	TSR
PSALM	105	20	TSR	PSALM	106	30	TSR	PSALM	116	4	TSR
PSALM	105	21	TSR	PSALM	106	31	TSR	PSALM	116	5	TSR
PSALM	105	22	TSR	PSALM	106	32	TSR	PSALM	116	6	TSR
PSALM	105	23	TSR	PSALM	106	33	TSR	PSALM	116	7	TSR
PSALM	105	24	TSR	PSALM	106	34	TSR	PSALM	116	8	TSR
PSALM	105	25	TSR	PSALM	106	35	TSR	PSALM	116	9	TSR
PSALM	105	26	TSR	PSALM	106	36	TSR	PSALM	116	10	TSR
PSALM	105	27	TSR	PSALM	106	37	TSR	PSALM	116	11	TSR
PSALM	105	28	TSR	PSALM	106	38	TSR	PSALM	116	12	TSR
PSALM	105	29	TSR	PSALM	106	39	TSR	PSALM	116	13	TSR
PSALM	105	30	TSR	PSALM	106	40	TSR	PSALM	116	14	TSR
PSALM	105	31	TSR	PSALM	106	41	TSR	PSALM	116	15	TSR
PSALM	105	32	TSR	PSALM	106	42	TSR	PSALM	116	16	TSR
PSALM	105	33	TSR	PSALM	106	43	TSR	PSALM	116	17	TSR
PSALM	105	34	TSR	PSALM	106	44	TSR	PSALM	116	18	TSR
PSALM	105	35	TSR	PSALM	106	45	TSR	PSALM	116	19	TSR
PSALM	105	36	TSR	PSALM	106	46	TSR	PSALM	118	5	TSR
PSALM	105	37	TSR	PSALM	107	4	TSR	PSALM	118	6	TSR
PSALM	105	38	TSR	PSALM	107	5	TSR	PSALM	118	10	TSR
PSALM	105	39	TSR	PSALM	107	6	TSR	PSALM	118	11	TSR
PSALM	105	40	TSR	PSALM	107	7	TSR	PSALM	118	12	TSR

PSALM	118	13	TSR								
PSALM	124	1	TSR								
PSALM	124	2	TSR								
PSALM	124	3	TSR								
PSALM	124	4	TSR								
PSALM	124	5	TSR								
PSALM	124	6	TSR								
PSALM	124	7	TSR								
PSALM	124	8	TSR								
PSALM	140	7	TSR								

PSALM	2	4	W	PSALM	17	3	W	PSALM	36	6	W
PSALM	2	5	W	PSALM	17	4	W	PSALM	36	7	W
PSALM	2	9	W	PSALM	17	15	W	PSALM	36	8	W
PSALM	3	2	W	PSALM	18	15	W	PSALM	36	9	W
PSALM	3	3	W	PSALM	18	25	W	PSALM	40	5	W
PSALM	4	7	W	PSALM	18	26	W	PSALM	40	17	W
PSALM	4	8	W	PSALM	18	27	W	PSALM	41	13	W
PSALM	5	3	W	PSALM	18	28	W	PSALM	42	1	W
PSALM	5	4	W	PSALM	18	29	W	PSALM	42	2	W
PSALM	5	5	W	PSALM	18	35	W	PSALM	42	5	W
PSALM	5	6	W	PSALM	18	36	W	PSALM	42	6	W
PSALM	5	7	W	PSALM	18	40	W	PSALM	42	7	W
PSALM	5	9	W	PSALM	18	43	W	PSALM	42	8	W
PSALM	5	12	W	PSALM	18	49	W	PSALM	42	9	W
PSALM	6	3	W	PSALM	20	5	W	PSALM	42	10	W
PSALM	6	4	W	PSALM	21	1	W	PSALM	42	11	W
PSALM	6	5	W	PSALM	21	8	W	PSALM	45	2	W
PSALM	6	6	W	PSALM	21	9	W	PSALM	45	3	W
PSALM	6	7	W	PSALM	21	10	W	PSALM	45	4	W
PSALM	6	8	W	PSALM	22	3	W	PSALM	45	5	W
PSALM	6	9	W	PSALM	22	8	W	PSALM	45	6	W
PSALM	6	10	W	PSALM	22	9	W	PSALM	45	7	W
PSALM	7	7	W	PSALM	22	10	W	PSALM	45	8	W
PSALM	7	8	W	PSALM	23	4	W	PSALM	45	9	W
PSALM	7	9	W	PSALM	23	5	W	PSALM	45	10	W
PSALM	8	1	W	PSALM	23	6	W	PSALM	45	11	W
PSALM	8	2	W	PSALM	24	1	W	PSALM	45	12	W
PSALM	8	3	W	PSALM	24	7	W	PSALM	45	13	W
PSALM	8	9	W	PSALM	24	8	W	PSALM	45	14	W
PSALM	9	1	W	PSALM	24	9	W	PSALM	45	15	W
PSALM	9	2	W	PSALM	25	1	W	PSALM	45	16	W
PSALM	9	3	W	PSALM	25	15	W	PSALM	45	17	W
PSALM	9	4	W	PSALM	26	1	W	PSALM	46	1	W
PSALM	9	5	W	PSALM	28	6	W	PSALM	46	2	W
PSALM	9	10	W	PSALM	28	7	W	PSALM	46	3	W
PSALM	9	14	W	PSALM	28	8	W	PSALM	46	4	W
PSALM	10	5	W	PSALM	30	1	W	PSALM	46	5	W
PSALM	10	14	W	PSALM	31	10	W	PSALM	46	6	W
PSALM	10	17	W	PSALM	32	1	W	PSALM	46	7	W
PSALM	10	18	W	PSALM	32	2	W	PSALM	46	8	W
PSALM	12	7	W	PSALM	32	6	W	PSALM	46	9	W
PSALM	13	5	W	PSALM	34	1	W	PSALM	46	10	W
PSALM	13	6	W	PSALM	34	2	W	PSALM	46	11	W
PSALM	15	1	W	PSALM	35	9	W	PSALM	47	1	W
PSALM	16	2	W	PSALM	35	10	W	PSALM	47	2	W
PSALM	16	3	W	PSALM	35	18	W	PSALM	47	3	W
PSALM	16	5	W	PSALM	35	27	W	PSALM	47	4	W
PSALM	16	10	W	PSALM	35	28	W	PSALM	47	5	W
PSALM	16	11	W	PSALM	36	5	W	PSALM	47	6	W

PSALM	47	7	W	PSALM	63	11	W	PSALM	72	19	W
PSALM	47	8	W	PSALM	65	1	W	PSALM	73	17	W
PSALM	47	9	W	PSALM	65	2	W	PSALM	73	18	W
PSALM	48	1	W	PSALM	65	3	W	PSALM	73	19	W
PSALM	48	2	W	PSALM	65	4	W	PSALM	73	20	W
PSALM	48	3	W	PSALM	65	5	W	PSALM	75	1	W
PSALM	48	4	W	PSALM	65	6	W	PSALM	76	4	W
PSALM	48	5	W	PSALM	65	7	W	PSALM	76	6	W
PSALM	48	6	W	PSALM	65	8	W	PSALM	76	7	W
PSALM	48	7	W	PSALM	65	9	W	PSALM	77	13	W
PSALM	48	8	W	PSALM	65	10	W	PSALM	77	14	W
PSALM	49	15	W	PSALM	65	11	W	PSALM	77	19	W
PSALM	50	1	W	PSALM	65	12	W	PSALM	81	1	W
PSALM	50	2	W	PSALM	65	13	W	PSALM	81	2	W
PSALM	50	3	W	PSALM	66	1	W	PSALM	81	3	W
PSALM	50	4	W	PSALM	66	2	W	PSALM	83	1	W
PSALM	50	5	W	PSALM	66	3	W	PSALM	84	2	W
PSALM	50	6	W	PSALM	66	4	W	PSALM	84	3	W
PSALM	52	9	W	PSALM	66	5	W	PSALM	84	4	W
PSALM	56	4	W	PSALM	66	6	W	PSALM	84	5	W
PSALM	56	9	W	PSALM	66	7	W	PSALM	84	6	W
PSALM	59	8	W	PSALM	66	8	W	PSALM	84	7	W
PSALM	59	9	W	PSALM	66	9	W	PSALM	84	8	W
PSALM	59	10	W	PSALM	66	10	W	PSALM	84	9	W
PSALM	60	4	W	PSALM	66	11	W	PSALM	84	10	W
PSALM	60	6	W	PSALM	66	12	W	PSALM	84	11	W
PSALM	60	7	W	PSALM	66	13	W	PSALM	84	12	W
PSALM	60	8	W	PSALM	66	14	W	PSALM	86	5	W
PSALM	60	9	W	PSALM	66	15	W	PSALM	86	8	W
PSALM	60	10	W	PSALM	66	16	W	PSALM	86	9	W
PSALM	60	12	W	PSALM	66	20	W	PSALM	86	10	W
PSALM	61	5	W	PSALM	68	7	W	PSALM	86	12	W
PSALM	61	6	W	PSALM	68	19	W	PSALM	86	13	W
PSALM	61	7	W	PSALM	68	26	W	PSALM	86	15	W
PSALM	61	8	W	PSALM	68	27	W	PSALM	87	3	W
PSALM	62	1	W	PSALM	68	29	W	PSALM	89	1	W
PSALM	62	2	W	PSALM	68	35	W	PSALM	89	2	W
PSALM	62	5	W	PSALM	69	5	W	PSALM	89	5	W
PSALM	62	12	W	PSALM	69	13	W	PSALM	89	6	W
PSALM	63	1	W	PSALM	69	34	W	PSALM	89	7	W
PSALM	63	2	W	PSALM	71	5	W	PSALM	89	8	W
PSALM	63	3	W	PSALM	71	6	W	PSALM	89	9	W
PSALM	63	4	W	PSALM	71	7	W	PSALM	89	10	W
PSALM	63	5	W	PSALM	71	17	W	PSALM	89	11	W
PSALM	63	6	W	PSALM	71	19	W	PSALM	89	12	W
PSALM	63	7	W	PSALM	71	20	W	PSALM	89	13	W
PSALM	63	8	W	PSALM	71	21	W	PSALM	89	14	W
PSALM	63	9	W	PSALM	71	22	W	PSALM	89	16	W
PSALM	63	10	W	PSALM	72	18	W	PSALM	89	17	W

PSALM	89	18	W	PSALM	96	3	W	PSALM	103	12	W
PSALM	89	19	W	PSALM	96	4	W	PSALM	103	13	W
PSALM	89	20	W	PSALM	96	5	W	PSALM	103	14	W
PSALM	89	21	W	PSALM	96	6	W	PSALM	103	15	W
PSALM	89	22	W	PSALM	96	7	W	PSALM	103	16	W
PSALM	89	23	W	PSALM	97	1	W	PSALM	103	17	W
PSALM	89	52	W	PSALM	97	2	W	PSALM	103	18	W
PSALM	90	1	W	PSALM	97	3	W	PSALM	103	19	W
PSALM	90	2	W	PSALM	97	4	W	PSALM	103	20	W
PSALM	90	3	W	PSALM	97	5	W	PSALM	103	21	W
PSALM	90	4	W	PSALM	97	6	W	PSALM	103	22	W
PSALM	90	5	W	PSALM	97	7	W	PSALM	104	1	W
PSALM	90	6	W	PSALM	98	1	W	PSALM	104	2	W
PSALM	90	7	W	PSALM	98	2	W	PSALM	104	3	W
PSALM	90	8	W	PSALM	98	3	W	PSALM	104	4	W
PSALM	90	9	W	PSALM	98	4	W	PSALM	104	5	W
PSALM	90	10	W	PSALM	98	5	W	PSALM	104	6	W
PSALM	90	11	W	PSALM	98	6	W	PSALM	104	7	W
PSALM	92	2	W	PSALM	98	7	W	PSALM	104	8	W
PSALM	92	3	W	PSALM	98	8	W	PSALM	104	9	W
PSALM	92	4	W	PSALM	98	9	W	PSALM	104	10	W
PSALM	92	5	W	PSALM	99	1	W	PSALM	104	11	W
PSALM	92	6	W	PSALM	99	2	W	PSALM	104	12	W
PSALM	92	7	W	PSALM	99	3	W	PSALM	104	13	W
PSALM	92	8	W	PSALM	99	4	W	PSALM	104	14	W
PSALM	92	9	W	PSALM	99	5	W	PSALM	104	15	W
PSALM	92	10	W	PSALM	99	6	W	PSALM	104	16	W
PSALM	92	11	W	PSALM	99	7	W	PSALM	104	17	W
PSALM	93	2	W	PSALM	99	8	W	PSALM	104	18	W
PSALM	93	3	W	PSALM	99	9	W	PSALM	104	19	W
PSALM	93	4	W	PSALM	100	1	W	PSALM	104	20	W
PSALM	93	5	W	PSALM	100	2	W	PSALM	104	21	W
PSALM	94	12	W	PSALM	100	3	W	PSALM	104	22	W
PSALM	94	13	W	PSALM	100	4	W	PSALM	104	23	W
PSALM	94	18	W	PSALM	100	5	W	PSALM	104	24	W
PSALM	94	19	W	PSALM	101	1	W	PSALM	104	25	W
PSALM	94	20	W	PSALM	102	12	W	PSALM	104	26	W
PSALM	94	21	W	PSALM	102	28	W	PSALM	104	27	W
PSALM	94	22	W	PSALM	103	1	W	PSALM	104	28	W
PSALM	94	23	W	PSALM	103	2	W	PSALM	104	29	W
PSALM	95	1	W	PSALM	103	3	W	PSALM	104	30	W
PSALM	95	2	W	PSALM	103	4	W	PSALM	104	31	W
PSALM	95	3	W	PSALM	103	5	W	PSALM	104	32	W
PSALM	95	4	W	PSALM	103	6	W	PSALM	104	33	W
PSALM	95	5	W	PSALM	103	7	W	PSALM	104	34	W
PSALM	95	6	W	PSALM	103	8	W	PSALM	104	35	W
PSALM	95	7	W	PSALM	103	9	W	PSALM	105	1	W
PSALM	96	1	W	PSALM	103	10	W	PSALM	105	2	W
PSALM	96	2	W	PSALM	103	11	W	PSALM	105	3	W

PSALM	106	1	W	PSALM	119	15	W	PSALM	119	98	W
PSALM	106	2	W	PSALM	119	16	W	PSALM	119	99	W
PSALM	106	48	W	PSALM	119	20	W	PSALM	119	100	W
PSALM	107	1	W	PSALM	119	23	W	PSALM	119	101	W
PSALM	108	1	W	PSALM	119	24	W	PSALM	119	102	W
PSALM	108	2	W	PSALM	119	30	W	PSALM	119	103	W
PSALM	108	3	W	PSALM	119	31	W	PSALM	119	104	W
PSALM	108	4	W	PSALM	119	32	W	PSALM	119	105	W
PSALM	108	10	W	PSALM	119	44	W	PSALM	119	106	W
PSALM	108	11	W	PSALM	119	45	W	PSALM	119	109	W
PSALM	109	30	W	PSALM	119	46	W	PSALM	119	110	W
PSALM	109	31	W	PSALM	119	47	W	PSALM	119	111	W
PSALM	111	1	W	PSALM	119	48	W	PSALM	119	112	W
PSALM	111	2	W	PSALM	119	50	W	PSALM	119	113	W
PSALM	111	3	W	PSALM	119	51	W	PSALM	119	114	W
PSALM	111	7	W	PSALM	119	52	W	PSALM	119	115	W
PSALM	112	1	W	PSALM	119	53	W	PSALM	119	118	W
PSALM	113	1	W	PSALM	119	54	W	PSALM	119	119	W
PSALM	113	2	W	PSALM	119	55	W	PSALM	119	120	W
PSALM	113	3	W	PSALM	119	56	W	PSALM	119	123	W
PSALM	113	4	W	PSALM	119	57	W	PSALM	119	126	W
PSALM	113	5	W	PSALM	119	58	W	PSALM	119	127	W
PSALM	113	6	W	PSALM	119	59	W	PSALM	119	128	W
PSALM	113	7	W	PSALM	119	60	W	PSALM	119	129	W
PSALM	113	8	W	PSALM	119	61	W	PSALM	119	130	W
PSALM	113	9	W	PSALM	119	62	W	PSALM	119	131	W
PSALM	115	17	W	PSALM	119	63	W	PSALM	119	136	W
PSALM	115	18	W	PSALM	119	64	W	PSALM	119	137	W
PSALM	117	1	W	PSALM	119	65	W	PSALM	119	138	W
PSALM	117	2	W	PSALM	119	67	W	PSALM	119	139	W
PSALM	118	1	W	PSALM	119	69	W	PSALM	119	140	W
PSALM	118	2	W	PSALM	119	70	W	PSALM	119	141	W
PSALM	118	3	W	PSALM	119	71	W	PSALM	119	142	W
PSALM	118	4	W	PSALM	119	72	W	PSALM	119	143	W
PSALM	118	19	W	PSALM	119	73	W	PSALM	119	145	W
PSALM	118	20	W	PSALM	119	74	W	PSALM	119	146	W
PSALM	118	21	W	PSALM	119	75	W	PSALM	119	147	W
PSALM	118	26	W	PSALM	119	81	W	PSALM	119	148	W
PSALM	118	27	W	PSALM	119	82	W	PSALM	119	150	W
PSALM	118	28	W	PSALM	119	83	W	PSALM	119	151	W
PSALM	118	29	W	PSALM	119	84	W	PSALM	119	152	W
PSALM	119	1	W	PSALM	119	89	W	PSALM	119	155	W
PSALM	119	2	W	PSALM	119	90	W	PSALM	119	156	W
PSALM	119	3	W	PSALM	119	91	W	PSALM	119	157	W
PSALM	119	9	W	PSALM	119	92	W	PSALM	119	158	W
PSALM	119	11	W	PSALM	119	93	W	PSALM	119	160	W
PSALM	119	12	W	PSALM	119	95	W	PSALM	119	161	W
PSALM	119	13	W	PSALM	119	96	W	PSALM	119	162	W
PSALM	119	14	W	PSALM	119	97	W	PSALM	119	163	W

PSALM	119	164	W	PSALM	132	6	W	PSALM	137	2	W
PSALM	119	165	W	PSALM	132	7	W	PSALM	137	3	W
PSALM	119	166	W	PSALM	132	8	W	PSALM	137	4	W
PSALM	119	167	W	PSALM	132	9	W	PSALM	137	5	W
PSALM	119	168	W	PSALM	132	10	W	PSALM	137	6	W
PSALM	119	171	W	PSALM	133	1	W	PSALM	138	1	W
PSALM	119	172	W	PSALM	133	2	W	PSALM	138	2	W
PSALM	119	174	W	PSALM	133	3	W	PSALM	138	3	W
PSALM	121	1	W	PSALM	134	1	W	PSALM	138	4	W
PSALM	121	2	W	PSALM	134	2	W	PSALM	138	5	W
PSALM	121	3	W	PSALM	134	3	W	PSALM	138	6	W
PSALM	121	4	W	PSALM	135	1	W	PSALM	138	7	W
PSALM	121	5	W	PSALM	135	2	W	PSALM	138	8	W
PSALM	121	6	W	PSALM	135	3	W	PSALM	139	1	W
PSALM	121	7	W	PSALM	135	4	W	PSALM	139	2	W
PSALM	121	8	W	PSALM	135	5	W	PSALM	139	3	W
PSALM	122	1	W	PSALM	135	6	W	PSALM	139	4	W
PSALM	122	2	W	PSALM	135	7	W	PSALM	139	5	W
PSALM	122	3	W	PSALM	135	8	W	PSALM	139	6	W
PSALM	122	4	W	PSALM	135	9	W	PSALM	139	7	W
PSALM	122	5	W	PSALM	135	10	W	PSALM	139	8	W
PSALM	122	7	W	PSALM	135	11	W	PSALM	139	9	W
PSALM	122	8	W	PSALM	135	12	W	PSALM	139	10	W
PSALM	122	9	W	PSALM	135	13	W	PSALM	139	11	W
PSALM	123	1	W	PSALM	135	14	W	PSALM	139	12	W
PSALM	123	2	W	PSALM	135	15	W	PSALM	139	13	W
PSALM	123	3	W	PSALM	135	16	W	PSALM	139	14	W
PSALM	125	1	W	PSALM	135	17	W	PSALM	139	15	W
PSALM	125	2	W	PSALM	135	18	W	PSALM	139	16	W
PSALM	125	3	W	PSALM	135	19	W	PSALM	139	17	W
PSALM	126	1	W	PSALM	135	20	W	PSALM	139	18	W
PSALM	126	2	W	PSALM	135	21	W	PSALM	139	19	W
PSALM	126	3	W	PSALM	136	1	W	PSALM	144	1	W
PSALM	126	5	W	PSALM	136	2	W	PSALM	144	2	W
PSALM	126	6	W	PSALM	136	3	W	PSALM	144	9	W
PSALM	130	3	W	PSALM	136	4	W	PSALM	144	10	W
PSALM	130	4	W	PSALM	136	10	W	PSALM	144	15	W
PSALM	130	5	W	PSALM	136	11	W	PSALM	145	1	W
PSALM	130	6	W	PSALM	136	12	W	PSALM	145	2	W
PSALM	130	7	W	PSALM	136	17	W	PSALM	145	3	W
PSALM	130	8	W	PSALM	136	18	W	PSALM	145	4	W
PSALM	131	1	W	PSALM	136	19	W	PSALM	145	5	W
PSALM	131	2	W	PSALM	136	20	W	PSALM	145	6	W
PSALM	131	3	W	PSALM	136	21	W	PSALM	145	7	W
PSALM	132	1	W	PSALM	136	22	W	PSALM	145	8	W
PSALM	132	2	W	PSALM	136	23	W	PSALM	145	9	W
PSALM	132	3	W	PSALM	136	24	W	PSALM	145	10	W
PSALM	132	4	W	PSALM	136	26	W	PSALM	145	11	W
PSALM	132	5	W	PSALM	137	1	W	PSALM	145	12	W

PSALM	145	13	W	PSALM	149	1	W				
PSALM	145	14	W	PSALM	149	2	W				
PSALM	145	15	W	PSALM	149	3	W				
PSALM	145	16	W	PSALM	149	4	W				
PSALM	145	17	W	PSALM	149	5	W				
PSALM	145	18	W	PSALM	149	6	W				
PSALM	145	19	W	PSALM	149	7	W				
PSALM	145	20	W	PSALM	149	8	W				
PSALM	145	21	W	PSALM	149	9	W				
PSALM	146	1	W	PSALM	150	1	W				
PSALM	146	2	W	PSALM	150	2	W				
PSALM	146	3	W	PSALM	150	3	W				
PSALM	146	4	W	PSALM	150	4	W				
PSALM	146	5	W	PSALM	150	5	W				
PSALM	146	6	W	PSALM	150	6	W				
PSALM	146	7	W								
PSALM	146	8	W								
PSALM	146	9	W								
PSALM	146	10	W								
PSALM	147	1	W								
PSALM	147	2	W								
PSALM	147	3	W								
PSALM	147	4	W								
PSALM	147	5	W								
PSALM	147	6	W								
PSALM	147	7	W								
PSALM	147	9	W								
PSALM	147	10	W								
PSALM	147	11	W								
PSALM	147	12	W								
PSALM	147	13	W								
PSALM	147	14	W								
PSALM	147	15	W								
PSALM	147	19	W								
PSALM	147	20	W								
PSALM	148	1	W								
PSALM	148	2	W								
PSALM	148	3	W								
PSALM	148	4	W								
PSALM	148	5	W								
PSALM	148	6	W								
PSALM	148	7	W								
PSALM	148	8	W								
PSALM	148	9	W								
PSALM	148	10	W								
PSALM	148	11	W								
PSALM	148	12	W								
PSALM	148	13	W								
PSALM	148	14	W